YANNIS RITSOS
AMONG HIS CONTEMPORARIES

MARJORIE CHAMBERS was born in Northern Ireland and educated at Trinity College Dublin and the Sorbonne. She taught Modern Greek Language and Literature at Queen's University Belfast. Her translations of Greek poetry, fiction and drama have been published in the U.S.A., Greece, England and the Republic of Ireland, and, apart from the Greek poetry in this volume (for details of previous publication, see the Copyright page), they include the following:

Kalamos and Acheron, a collection of short stories by Christoforos Milionis
(Kedros Publishers, Athens 1990).

My Life in the Furnace by Panayotis Tranoulis (Pella Publishing, New York, 2005).

And from Colenso Books (2015), there is her translation of
Iakovos Kambanellis' *Three Plays:*
The courtyard of wonders — The four legs of the table — Ibsenland.

She has also published critical articles on some of the Greek authors she has translated:

"Ritsos and Greek mythology" in *Hermathena: A Trinity College Dublin Review* 153 (1992); republished in *Themata Logotechnias* (*Literary Topics*) 42 (2009).

"Ritsos in Belfast" in *Themata Logotechnias* 5 (March–June 1997)

"Translating Millionis" in *Themata Logotechnias* 23 (May–August 2003)

(The two articles on Ritsos are included in the present volume, together with a third which has not been published before.)

YANNIS RITSOS

AMONG HIS CONTEMPORARIES

TWENTIETH-CENTURY GREEK POETRY

TRANSLATED BY
MARJORIE CHAMBERS

Including poems by Yannis Ritsos, George Vafopoulos,
Nikos Gatsos, Nikiforos Vrettakos, Miltos Sachtouris
and Yannis Kondos
with three essays on Ritsos by Marjorie Chambers

COLENSO BOOKS
2018

This collection of translations first published November 2018
by
Colenso Books
68 Palatine Road, London N16 8ST, UK
colensobooks@gmail.com
Reprinted with minor corrections February 2019

ISBN 978-0-9928632-9-6

Copyright © 2018 Marjorie Chambers

Many of the translations were first published in *The Charioteer: An Annual Review of Modern Greek Culture*, Pella Publishing, New York (now discontinued), as follows:
some of the poems by Yannis Ritsos in No 29/30 (1987–88)
all of the poems by George Vafopoulos in No 31/32 (1989–90)
all of the poems by Nikiforos Vrettakos in No 33/34 (1991–92)
all of the poems by Nikos Gatsos in No 36 (1995–96)
all of the poems by Miltos Sachtouris in No 37/38 (1997–99).

The translations of *The Moonlight Sonata*, *Farewell* and *The prison tree and the women*
first appeared in the volume Yannis Ritsos, *Prison poems*, published by
The Goldsmith Press, Newbridge, Co. Kildaire, Ireland (2001), and are republished
here with the permission of The Goldsmith Press.
The translation of *Farewell* had previously appeared in
The Modern Greek Studies Yearbook (University of Minnesota), Vol. 7 (1991).

The translation of "It could be a Bergman film" by Yannis Kondos
was first published in *Stand Magazine* vol. 1, No. 3 (September 1999).

The translations of the other poems by Yannis Kondos, together with "Ajax", *Love poems*
and poems from *Responses* by Yannis Ritsos are all published here for the first time.
Permission to publish the translations from the work of Yannis Kondos
was given by Argyris Paloukas.
Permission to publish the new translations from the work of Yannis Ritsos
was given by Eleftheria Ritsou-Glezou.

The image on the cover is a painting on stone by Yannis Ristsos
reproduced by permission of Eleftheria Ritsou-Glezou.

CONTENTS

INTRODUCTION ... ix
    Yannis Ritsos ... ix
    George Vafopoulos ... xiii
    Nikos Gatsos ... xiii
    Nikiforos Vrettakos ... xiv
    Miltos Sachtouris ... xv
    Yannis Kondos ... xvi

YANNIS RITSOS (1909–1990) ... 1
    My sister's song (1937) ... 3
    The March of the Ocean (1940) ... 27
    The Moonlight Sonata (1956) ... 57
    Farewell (1957) ... 65
    The prison tree and the women (1963) ... 79
    from *Twelve poems on Cavafy* (1963) ... 87
        The poet's room ... 87
    from *The fourth dimension* (1972) ... 89
        Ajax ... 89
    Love poems (1981): all untitled ... 101
        "You've come back from the market" ... 101
        "Erotic sleep after love" ... 101
        "Your body on the beach" ... 102
        "Therefore I turn the stone" ... 102
        "The sunset gleamed" ... 103
        "You threw off the sheet" ... 103
        "A large rose climbs companionless" ... 104
        "Put your bare foot on the paper" ... 104
    from *Responses* (1987) ... 105
        The blood ... 105
        He with the hat ... 105
        Fishing village ... 106
        Sudden change ... 106
        Justification ... 107
        One night ... 107
        Consolatory ... 108
        Musical substitute ... 108
        These ... 109
        The hour of waiting ... 109

GEORGE VAFOPOULOS (1903–1996) — 111

from *The offering* (1938) — 113
- The calendar — 113

from *Songs of resurrection* (1948) — 115
- Thou in me — 115

from *The big night and the window* (1959) — 119
- Scales — 119
- The hedgehog — 120
- Fear — 121

from *The sequel* (1977) — 123
- First symphony in red and white — 123

NIKOS GATSOS (1911–1992) — 125

Amorgos (1943) — 127

from *Lend silken threads to the wind* (1994) — 135
- Spanish rhapsody — 135
- "To bring you herbs and myrrh" (untitled) — 136
- "What can you say?" (untitled) — 136
- Take your ring — 137
- "Beat tambourines on the slopes" (untitled) — 138
- "Patient horses wait in the courtyard" (untitled) — 138
- Orange tree of Aegina — 139
- "Blood, blood, blood" (untitled) — 139
- 'Down in the white sea" (untitled) — 139
- "Because I took you" (untitled) — 140
- A summer night — 140
- "Ah, what a withered meadow!" (untitled) — 140
- "A ruined bell-tower" (untitled) — 141

NIKIFOROS VRETTAKOS (1912–1991) — 143

from *Gifts in abeyance* (1986) — 145
- Euphoria — 145
- Whatever happens — 145
- Short ode — 146
- Tree planting — 146
- The Greek language — 146
- The field of words — 147
- The Ten Commandments — 147
- The eyes of insects — 148
- The tulip — 148
- The decay of hands — 148
- Memory of lost blood — 149
- Out of superfluity — 149

from *Chorus* (1988)	151
The cloud	151
Fourteen poems for the same mountain	151
Creation	157
The workshop	157
Poetry	158
Epigram of life	158
Chorus	158
Neither	159
Pascal exaltation	159
MILTOS SACHTOURIS (1919–2005)	161
from *The forgotten woman* (1945)	163
The dream	163
Beauty	164
The three lovers	165
from *Ballads* (1948)	167
The dead man in our lives Ioannis Veniamin d'Arkozi	167
Observatory	168
The nightmare	169
The gifts	170
Deep mine	171
The sky	172
Sometimes the women	173
It isn't Oedipus	174
from *With face to the wall* (1952)	175
On the nature of the beast	175
Experiments for the repetition of night	176
The scene	177
Nostalgia returns	178
The telephone	179
The carnival	180
Metamorphosis	181
YANNIS KONDOS (1943–1996)	183
from *At the coming of day* (1992)	185
An end to journeys	185
Twenty-four-hour news	186
Mistaken identities	187
The anatomist	188
The traveller with the black box	189
from *The nothing athlete* (1997)	191
It could be a Bergman film	191
Bronze Age	192

[Yannis Kondos, from *The nothing athlete*, continued]
    Absentminded with love *or* What does Emily
        Dickinson want from us?   193
    Pedagogics   194
    Rural country   195
    For schoolfellows   196
    What became of Charles Dickens's children   196

ESSAYS BY MARJORIE CHAMBERS   199
    Ritsos and Greek mythology (1992)   201
    Ritsos in Belfast (1997)   217
    Ritsos in Dublin (2017)   223

Index of titles and first lines   227

INTRODUCTION

The older Greek poets in this collection experienced the troubled decades before the Second World War, the Axis Occupation of Greece and the Civil War which followed (1946–49). The disillusionment prevalent during the post-war decades was shared by the younger generation of poets, represented here by Yannis Kondos. Perhaps the best known of these poets internationally is Yannis Ritsos.

YANNIS RITSOS (1909–1990)

Yannis Ritsos was born in Monemvasia, into a well-to-do landowning family which lost its wealth, partly as a consequence of the 1921–23 war with Turkey, and partly due to his father's gambling debts.

Ritsos' sister, Loula Ritsou-Glezou, in her book *Ta paidika chronia tou adelfou mou Yanni Ritsou* (*The childhood and youth of my brother Yannis Ritsos*) describes their troubled childhood, during which they lost their mother and their brother to tuberculosis. When Ritsos and his sister moved to Athens, after attending secondary school in Yithion, he too succumbed to tuberculosis and spent some years of his youth in sanatoria.

During the Second World War and the Civil War Ritsos became involved in the leftist cause. He was active in the cultural section of EAM, the National Liberation Front, and took part in the morale-boosting campaign for ELAS, the National Popular Liberation Army. Because of these political activities he was interned in the island prisons of Limnos, Makronisos, and Ai-Stratis between 1948 and 1952.

Later, under the Junta, the Colonels' regime of 1967–74, he was imprisoned on the islands of Yaros and Leros. Following international pressure, he was freed from Leros and placed under house arrest on Samos in 1968. He returned to Athens under surveillance in 1970.

During the last decades of his life Ritsos was active in the cause of world peace. In 1977 he received the Lenin Prize for Peace and in 1979 he was awarded the International Peace Prize from the World Peace Organisation. In 1986 he was a founder member with Mikis Theodorakis, of the Greek–Turkish Friendship Society. Shortly before he died Ritsos said: "There must be peace throughout the world because you cannot yourself be at peace when your brother is being wronged."

Ritsos wrote 120 collections of poems, ranging in style from the traditional to the surrealist. Growing up in Monemvasia he was well acquainted with the tone and rhythms of the Orthodox liturgy and Greek folk song. He also wrote nine volumes of prose and various translations of Eastern European poets.

My sister's song
In *My sister's song* (1937, pp. 3–26), personal grief is fused with historical awareness.

INTRODUCTION

This poem is one of the trilogy of symphonic poems including *Spring Symphnoy* (1938) and *The march of the ocean* (1940, pp. 27–56) which indirectly expressed the spirit of resistance against the Metaxas dictatorship in Greece and the rise of fascism in Europe. From *My sister's song* the lines beginning "Here is the trophy of life" and ending "I open my arms and accept the irresistible" (p. 23) became well-known as a slogan of resistance. The sun, to which these lines refer, symbolizes the steadfast belief of Ritsos in the redemptive power of poetry and in man's ability, no matter what the circumstances, to respond to the irresistible call of life, to take the ascending path towards "a more substantial freedom". He has also said, "The way towards the sun has no return."

My sister's song also reflects the hardships the poet and his sister Loula suffered together when they came to work in Athens, after leaving school in Yithion. The poem was prompted by the rapid deterioration of Loula's mental condition. Ritsos emerges from the searing grief of his personal Calvary to respond finally to the irresistible call to life and the redemptive power of poetry, both symbolised by the sun, a dominant image in his work. His victory over despair, though, is not easily won. This is a bitter journey towards the light in the midst of darkness and is therefore a deeply moving testimony to man's heroic spirit.

The Moonlight Sonata

Ritsos' international reputation came with the publication of *The Moonlight Sonata* (pp. 57–64) in 1956. Ritsos himself mentioned to me in 1986 that this poem had been translated many times. The elderly woman, alone in the decaying house, suffers as a prisoner of a past from which she cannot free herself, despite her efforts to relate to a present from which she feels alienated. *The Moonlight Sonata* also reflects the poet's childhood experience of the demise of his own privileged land-owning class and its values, and the decay of his family home in Monemvasia. For the first time Ritsos uses the dramatic monologue, a device which, in this instance, heightens the tension between the persistent and fatal attraction — from the viewpont of the Left — of selfish individualism and its lack of relevance in a changing society. *The Moonlight Sonata* also reflects the general disillusionment in Greece which, despite an appearance of stability, seemed to have lost direction. The detainees, released from the camps in 1952–53, had endured the destruction of their hopes, and were then obliged to come to terms with a society marked by the growth of an avid materialism. The dancing bear in the poem symbolises a Greece exhausted by the sufferings of her recent past, and having neither the strength nor the will to emerge from the humiliating neo-colonial condition in which she found herself. Like the dancing bear, with which she identifies, the elderly woman also lacks the strength and the will to free herself from the impasse in which she suffers.

Farewell

Farewell (pp. 65–78) deals with that predominant theme in Greek poetry: death and freedom. The poem refers to an incident in the history of Cyprus. The Greek Civil War was not long ended when Greek Cypriots broached the question of *Enosis*

("Union" with Greece) in 1950. Britain was reluctant to accede to this demand, which was fiercely opposed by the Turkish minority in Cyprus. As a consequence EOKA (National Organization of Cypriot Combatants) began a campaign against the British in the island, under the guerrilla leader General Grivas. The crisis deepened when the Cypriot religious and political leader, Archbishop Makarios, was arrested by the British and exiled to the Seychelles Islands.

It is curious, on the face of it, that Grivas, who was notoriously anti-Communist, should have appointed as his second-in-command a man whose sympathies appear to have been towards the Left. Grigoris Afxendiou, who was the most competent of the EOKA leaders, commanded a small detachment in the Troodos area. During the prolonged siege of the cave at Machairas Monastery he displayed remarkable courage.

Ritsos, using the monologue form again, imagines the thoughts of such a man face-to-face with death. Indeed the poet was himself a man of great courage, having faced the prospect of death on more than one occasion, notably in the Makronisos internment camp. At one stage he was given twenty-four hours to make up his mind to sign the "repentance statement", but, despite evidence of the brutal punishments inflicted on others who had not signed, he refused to renounce his work or his ideals. Ritsos clearly identifies with his protagonist in the dilemma in which he finds himself. The poem is a loving and convincing portrayal of Afxendiou, who represents the indomitable spirit of the Greek nation. In Ritsos' mind Afxendiou also becomes a Christ-like figure, a spokesman for reconciliation: "brotherhood for us and for all men is not impossible. / Here differences will vanish in a smile" (p. 76).

The prison tree and the women

While the sun of faith shines with dazzling light in *Farewell*, a more modest heroism gently radiates faith in *The prison tree and the women* (1963, pp. 79–85), a verse drama written in Prague in 1962. It was inspired by an exhibition of woodcuts by Zizi Makri, a lifelong friend of the poet. She was imprisoned for unspecified reasons in the Averof Women's Prison in Athens in 1962–63. The actress Olymbia Papadouka was also a prisoner there from 1947 to 1950. She had been, with Ritsos, a member of the Athens People's Theatre, founded by EAM in Trikkala in 1945. In her book on the Averof prison Papadouka describes how the women prisoners, from all walks of life, used their various skills to help one another maintain dignity and sanity in conditions that were always degrading. Activities of prison life are described touchingly and humourously through song and dance. In her book there is a photograph of the prison yard, with a huge palm tree in the middle. Zizi Makri told me on the telephone from Budapest that this tree was the only living thing in Averof and therefore meant so much to the women prisoners. She described how they used to stroll and dance around it to lift their spirit. In the poem the tree is the focal point, a symbol of the undefeated human spirit. The words "and green leaves peep out of Mary's hair..." (p. 85) recall the regenerative powers associated with the image of the Byzantine Virgin. Whereas *The Moonlight Sonata* reveals the poet's understanding of how the human will can be corroded by time and memory, *The prison tree and the women* expresses the conviction that this dilemma can be resolved. The human spirit can survive if we remain conscious of the struggle for freedom and respond to its call.

Ajax

"Ajax" (pp. 89–99) was included in the collection *The fourth dimension* published in 1972. In the *Iliad*, while Achilles sulks in his tent after the quarrel with Agamemnon over the slave-woman Briseis, Ajax, the bulwark of the Achaians, is prominent in the battle against the Trojans, responding eagerly to frequent pleas for help. He is often referred to as fighting with "impetuous valour". He hinders the Trojans from reaching the Greek ships — while being continuously attacked by them. He succeeds in driving Hector away, and later, while defending the ships, wounds him with a stone. Ajax urges the Greeks to save their ships by hand-to-hand fighting. He and his half-brother, the illegitimate Tevkros, who are devoted to each other, fend off the Trojans as Menelaos and others carry off Patroclos' body to be buried.

During the funeral games in honour of Patroclos, Ajax wrestles with Odysseus. It's decided that there is no winner, and both take equal prizes. Ajax fights Diomedes in a duel. They share the armour of the Trojan Sarpedon — but Achilles also gives Diomedes the sword of Asteropaios. The Iliad ends with the slaying of Hector by Achilles.

In Sophocles' *Ajax*, Achilles's armour, the reward for valiant service, is given, not to Ajax, but to Odysseus by vote. Ajax, demented by jealousy and a burning sense of injustice, is about to kill Agamemnon and Menelaos when the goddess Athena intervenes, deflecting his rage towards the penned animals — the unassigned booty of the Greeks — making him believe they are his hated enemies, notably Odysseus. He rounds up the ones he hasn't slaughtered, and ties one of the rams to a post in his tent, and flogs it to death.

When Ajax comes to his senses, he is overcome with shame, and talks of killing himself. His captive wife Tecmessa pleads with him not to abandon herself and their son to slavery. He appears in the end to be very calm, but goes off and kills himself by falling on his sword (given to him by Hector).

In the second part of the play, there is a dispute between Agamemnon and Menelaos and Tevkros about the disposal of Ajax's body; Agamemnon and Menelaos and the Greek army in general regard him as a traitor whose body should be left to rot. Tevkros recalls how Menelaos cheated Ajax by "rigging votes against him", and reminds them of Ajax's unselfish and brave deeds, but they are unmoved. The chorus too is concerned that Ajax, in his overweening pride in his physical strength, lost all sense of self-control. When leaving Salamina for Troy, he declared to his dismayed father Telamon that he would win glory and honour on his own account — not with God beside him. And to the goddess Athena, who during the battle was showing him where best to fight, he suggested that she assist the Greeks who really needed her help: "The line won't break where I am in command."

In skilful argument Odysseus appeals to a sense of justice in Agamemnon and Menelaos, and persuades them to permit Tevkros to bury the body with due ceremony — acknowledging Ajax as "the bravest man he ever saw" — the best after Achilles.

INTRODUCTION

In the self-awareness of the characters in *The fourth dimension* Ritsos echoes Sophocles whose characters are responsible for their own personal fate. In Ritsos' poems the implication is that we are *also* responsible for the effects of whatever dispensation we have created.

Ritsos' monologue opens with Ajax prostrate among the animals he has slaughtered in a paranoiac frenzy, believing them to be his hated enemies, Agamemnon, Menelaos, Odysseus, and the other Greek warriors, mocking him — having treated him unjustly, by rewarding Odysseus with the dead Achilles' armour, which he believes should be his alone, by virtue of his frequently outstanding bravery in battle.

The tension in this poem is focused on Ajax's struggle to emerge from his mental chaos, to achieve balance. He vacillates throughout between bitterness at the unjust behaviour of the Greek leaders in exploiting and cheating him, and the realisation that he has wasted his life chasing vainglory in the fields of battle. In the end, Ajax kills himself, but not, as in Sophocles, through shame and despair at being deprived of the *kleos* or glory which was rightfully his.

In Sophocles's play, there is a sense of satisfaction that Ajax will be buried, that his achievements are acknowledged, that justice has been done, thanks to the skilful arguments of Odysseus; in Ritsos' poem there is a tragic sense of a wasted life, and an aura of utter loneliness surrounding his protagonist.

The claustrophobic atmosphere of the monologue form intensifies Ajax's loneliness and the bleak sense of alienation. His wife Tecmessa is a silent, helpless witness to his mental turmoil. Here, there is no Odysseus to argue for justice, no Tevkros, his beloved half-brother, to plead his achievements and bravery, to bury him, or to protect his wife and son. Ajax calls out to Tevkros — but there is no reply. In his final remarks to Tecmessa to whom he never refers by name, he says (p. 96), "I'm going to wash myself and wash my sword — and perhaps I'll find a man to talk to." Ritsos would have agreed with Sophocles that we are alone; there is no *deus ex machina*, so to speak, that will reveal to us the meaning of our existence. However, Ritsos never lost faith that we are capable of creating a society that could aspire to the safe haven which does not exist in the world of Sophocles.

As in the other monologues in *The fourth dimension*, the characters, notably Agamemnon, have had glimpses, in the throes of action, of the possibility of living in harmony with the world, of being a whole human being — of entering into what Ritsos refers to as "the fourth dimension"; he would very probably have approved of Vaclav Havel's first presidential speech (1990) in which he dreams of "a humane republic ... of a republic of well-rounded people, because without such it is impossible to solve any of our problems".

During a BBC television programme on Yannis Ritsos shortly before he died, an interviewee, in paying tribute to the poet, expressed the love his poetry had inspired in the Greek people: "He will always be a special person for Greece, bound up with the memories of freedom and independence, justice and the ideals of the Greek people, for which we have all fought side by side." An even more perceptive interviewee said: "If we had more like *him* things would be different for the whole world."

INTRODUCTION

GEORGE VAFOPOULOS (1903–1996)

After the Vafopoulos family moved from Serbia to territory newly acquired by Greece at the end of the Balkan Wars of 1912–13 — eventually settling in Thessaloniki in 1917 — they experienced a decline in their fortunes.

Known as "The Poet of Thessaloniki" George Vafopoulos did much to transform "this intellectual wasteland" as he referred to it, into a vibrant city of culture. From 1939 to 1964 he was Director of the Municipal Public Library of Thessaloniki. He became the editor of the periodical "Macedonian Letters" and was a member of a group which edited "Macedonian Days". He was general secretary of the Thessaloniki State Theatre and member of the State Theatre of Northern Greece. He also founded the Vafopoulos Cultural Centre.

Among the accolades he received were the Academy of Athens Ourani Award, the City of Thessaloniki Order of Merit, and the title Commander of the Order of the Phoenix.

Apart from his eight collections of poetry Vafopoulos wrote a play, short stories and essays, and *Selides aftoviografias* (*Pages of an autobiography*).

The image of night pervades his existentialist poems. Poised between human suffering, loneliness, and despair, and the desire to reach the light of hope Vafopoulos comes to terms with mortality, which is so very real to him — beyond existentialist posturing. The poem "The calendar" (pp. 113–14) refers to the death of his first wife which, at the age of thirty-two, brought him face to face with death for the first time.

The poem "Thou in me" (pp. 115–18) eloquently expresses his emergence from despair and fear of death through his Christian faith. This faith is sorely tried however, in the later, very moving poem "First symphony in red and white" (pp. 123–4), written in 1973, during the rule of the Colonels (1967–74), after students revolted and occupied the Polytechnic in Athens. The government's aggressive reaction to this event would seem to have reawakened, for the poet, memories of the terrible experiences suffered by the Greeks during the previous decades.

Ultimately, however, Vafopoulos does manage to achieve in his poems the light of hope and some respite from the fear of death.

NIKOS GATSOS (1911–1992)

Nikos Gatsos was born in the village of Asea, near Tripolis. He studied classics, history, and philosophy at the University of Athens. As a young man he contributed regularly to literary journals, and later worked for several years as a writer–director of plays for the Hellenic Broadcasting Corporation. He was also a distinguished translator of plays by Jean Genet, Garcia Lorca, Tennessee Williams, Eugene O'Neill, and August Stringberg, among others. His translations were performed at the National Greek Theatre and the Arts Theatre where he greatly influenced the director Karolos Koun.

While growing up in the countryside he became immersed in Greek folk songs and in the poetry of Solomos, Palamas, and Sikelianos who all wrote in the demotic or spoken language. These influences are apparent in the naturalism of his expression.

Gatsos was thirty-two years old when his long poem *Amorgos* (pp. 127–33) was first published in 1943. Amorgos is the name of one of the Cyclades islands. The poet never lived on an island, and never visited Amorgos; the place therefore would seem to have for him a symbolic significance, representing the whole world.

It was probably from his study of philosophy that Gatsos developed the stoical attitude towards the traumatic experience of the Axis Occupation that he was living through when he wrote *Amorgos*. In that poem he implies that from time immemorial man has endured temporary episodes of tragedy and suffering which are overcome by a refusal to yield to despair. ("do not become FATE", p. 127) Man must look towards the sea, towards the struggle for freedom and justice.

His dignified stance against the slavery imposed by the Occupation is nurtured in the poem by the combination of surrealistic images with the simplicity and restraint of folk song. However, Gatsos does not offer an easy optimism; he could not have failed to foresee the Civil War that was to follow the withdrawal of the Germans in 1944. By the end of "Amorgos" the sea, beckoning towards the light of hope, has been drained away. But, for Gatsos, what will always remain will be the beauty of poetry and the power it has to remind us all of our triumphs over disaster throughout the centuries.

For reasons unknown he published no poems after *Amorgos*, which has been translated into many languages. Despite the influence this poem had on the younger generation of poets, and the generally positive and fascinated reaction to it, he confined himself to writing dozens of beautiful lyrics that were set to music by Hadzidakis, Theodorakis, and Xarchakos, though he also left behind a few fragments of unpublished poems, which were collected and published in 1994 with the title, *Lend silken threads to the wind* (pp. 135–41). These fragments resonate with the sadness of folk song.

NIKIFOROS VRETTAKOS (1912–1991)

Nikiforos Vrettakos was born in Krokeës, near Sparta. He worked in a factory and as a clerk, civil servant, and literary editor for magazines and newspapers. He served in the Greek–Italian War (1940–41) and was afterwards involved in the National Resistance to the Axis Occupation. Vrettakos produced over forty collections of poetry and several works of prose. He was awarded five national prizes, among them the Greek State Poetry Prize (twice), as well as three international prizes. He was also nominated for the Nobel Prize. Vrettakos was honorary chairman of the Greek Writers' Guild and Chairman of the Greek Pen Club, and was elected to the Academy of Athens in 1987. In 1991 he received an honorary degree from the School of Philosophy, Athens University. His poems have been translated into many European languages, as well as Japanese, Hindi, Arabic, and Turkish.

In contrast to George Vafopoulous, Nikiforos Vrettakos is never far from his

Christian faith. In an interview in 1990 with Antonio Fosteris and Aristotle Michopoulos he said that "a prerequisite for peace can only be love for the human being that is becoming lost". While lamenting, in that interview, "the crippled moral dimension" of the world he nevertheless had faith in poetry as a "divine word". His contemplation of his beloved Mount Taïyetos — the subject of his "Fourteen poems to the same mountain" (pp. 151–7) — is permeated by his conviction that people can be in harmony with nature and therefore with one another.

In view of his previous despair and disillusionment during the troubled decades of the 1930s and 1940s in Greece and in the rest of Europe, his emergence from that experience, expressed with such radiant eloquence in the poems from the collections *Gifts in abeyance* (pp. 145–9) and *Chorus* (pp. 151–9) is truly inspiring.

MILTOS SACHTOURIS (1919–2005)

Miltos Sachtouris was born in Athens. His great-grandfather, Yorgos Sachtouris was one of the admirals in the Greek War of Independence in the 1820s. Urged by his father, who was a judge, Miltos enrolled as a law student at the University of Athens. When his father died he abandoned his legal studies and took care of his mentally ill mother until she died in 1955.

Sachtouris published twenty-one collections of poems and received three State Prizes for his poetry, among them the Grand State Literature Prize in 2003. Like Gatsos, he was influenced by Greek folk song, but unlike the older poet's studied nonchalance in his use of surrealism, there is practically no light coming through the relentlessly dark surrealistic imagery in the poetry of Sachtouris. His poems reflect what the dramatist Iakovos Kambanellis refers to in the foreword to his play "The Courtyard of Wonders" as "the psychological disintegration which followed the Civil War". The sense of alienation among friends and former acquaintances, which Sachtouris also expresses in these poems, would be inevitable under such circumstances. Sachtouris sees man as greedy, self-destructive, and irredeemably savage. Nor is there any consolation in love, which is forever elusive. His poems, in contrast with those of the previous poets in the present volume, scarcely offer the light of hope. Perhaps by recreating in his relentlessly black imagery the appalling experience he lived through, Sachtouris is attempting to exorcise it.

One example of the savagery and suffering during the Civil War is conveyed in "The Carnival" (p. 180). This poem echoes an event which occurred during that time. Christoforos Milionis, in his book *Akrokeravnia* (the name of a mountain) describes a scene in a town during the Apokria or pre-Lenten celebrations. The townspeople are thoroughly enjoying themselves, dancing and singing, when their attention is drawn to the police barracks. Two very drunken policemen are riding on a donkey. The crowd is amused by their floundering journey up the steps to the balcony of the barracks. Suddenly, one of them pulls out of his bag, a human head, which he triumphantly holds aloft by its long hair. The crowd is stunned into silence. It is the head of a leftist partisan who is the son of one of the townspeople. Christoforos

Milionis quotes the last line of "The Carnival" at the head of the chapter.

The only glimpse of hope is in the prose poem "The Nightmare" (p. 169). The young girl is referred to as "Seashore and Sunday", the name bringing to mind Greece's extensive coastline and implying reverence for Greece as the cradle of wetern civilisation.

At the end of the poem the girl is dead but her pitch-black clothes have been exchanged for a pure white dress. She is blood-soaked but with a green twig in her mouth — an image suggesting that Greece will survive again — survive as she always has survived the numerous savage invasions throughout the centuries.

YANNIS KONDOS (1943–2015)

Yannis Kondos was born in Eyion in the Peloponnese, the year before the Axis Occupation ended and the Civil War became widespread. After studying economics in Athens he worked for many years with the Hellenic Broadcasting Corporation and taught in a drama school. He also worked as an editor for a publisher. In 1973 he was placed on the Ford Civil List and was awarded the State Prize for Poetry in 1998.

First published in 1964 Yannis Kondos produced thirteen volumes of poetry, and wrote essays on Greek poets, writers, and painters. His poetry has been translated into the chief European languages. In 1978 two selections of his poems were published in English — namely *Mercurial Time* translated by Yannis Goumas and *Danger in the Streets* translated by Yannis Stathatos. In 1980 some of his poems were set to music by the composer Nikos Kollitsis.

Yannis Kondos, like many poets of his generation, conveys a reaction against official myth, ancestor worship and the didactic ideology that was manifested during the rule of the Junta (1967–74). The disenchanted tone in Kondos's poetry leans often towards irony.

Marjorie Chambers
Holywood, Co. Down, November 2017

YANNIS RITSOS

(1909–1990)

YANNIS RITSOS

My sister's song

To my sister LOULA

In the distorted mirrors
    of tears
is shattered the calm face
    of eternity
and yet we hear within us still
    the murmur of tranquillity.

My sister
I should have stood upright
against the sun
and raised the column of my verses
towards the blue expanse
that you might walk in the evenings,
smiling beside Eurydice
under the star-filled skies
of unending summers.
But, my sister,
I can do no more.
Infinity has smashed
its bright arc
on my brow
and I spin
in the eternal Moment
shattered and bewildered.
My voice has foundered.
Thought has plucked
its last flowers.
With sobs only
I utter your song.
Neither pain nor ecstasy
dare with bleeding lips
stammer your name.

— ◆ —

On the verdure of heaven
Ruth kneels
to pray at your feet.
The white doves
of childhood dreams
fly low in the plains
of your smile.
The musings of sages
never climbed
to the edges
of your venerable greatness.
Poets who have dissolved in the light
acknowledge in the light of your face
the emptiness of verses.
Only the great Silence
with a lily in her hands
gently touches your bent back
which has raised to God's bosom
the cries of men,
while the dark blue
star-weeping nights
in contrition cease to move.
My sister,
I fold my wings
I bend down
and kiss
the tips or your bare feet.
Grant that my mind may be calmed
that I may sing the hymn fit
for you, my sister,
sister of all the world.

— ◆ —

Your white hands
that covered our wounds with myrrh
now writhe behind your back
on the cross of your body
as if they were, my sister,
the hands of robbers.

MY SISTER'S SONG

Your thin body is entwined
in the grey mantle of frenzy.
Your eyes remain
empty glass citadels
where wander
lost ghosts of the past.
My sister,
how could you abandon me at midnight
to seek without a lamp
to find the traces
of your lost footsteps?
Plunge me also
into the same dark
that I may not hear the clarion
of your cries
that count the countless tombs.
Blast into infinity
my eyes
that I may not see
your bound hands.
Everywhere I turn
I see only you.
I entreat
the kindness of beauty
to bestow on me a drop of dew.
But no-one answers
the supplications
of vanquished people.
Yellow dust
from dead roses
snowed on the gardens.
The silent shore
withdrew in the twilight
and Spring fell asleep
its bright face
hidden in its hands.
Where is silence now
with its pure slumbers
its frozen trances
its faded roses?

— ◆ —

My sister,
I am no longer a poet
I do not deign to be a poet.
I am a maimed ant
that has lost its way
in boundless night.
I stir the embers
of burnt-out Aprils
and do not find a spark
to light the old fire.
You have weighed
the treasures of centuries
in your thin palm.
You have pulled down mountains
where poets rested.
And I, I am no longer a poet.
I know
that poets
do not besmirch
the ivory towers of cities
with their tears.
They keep watch,
their gaze level and unclouded
that they may count
the shimmerings of the light
and the pulsations of the universe.
But I,
my sister, I keep watch
counting your heartbeats
and your breaths.
I stand, a dark tower,
among crashing lightning bolts
and touch, unhesitating, the sword blades.
The arcs of light have faded
beneath your eyelids.
Nothing else lives
outside the mournful circle
your eyes trace on the world.
I do not want

the drums of triumph
to proclaim my glory
in the woods of spring.
Your smile
is enough for me.
The fountain of your eyes
can quench my thirst
and make my life blossom.

— ◆ —

I had a bright tunic
that warmed my hours.
I had the company of verses
that talked to me at nights
of triumphant campaigns.
Sitting silent and alone
on those lost mornings,
serene I pitched my tent
and there would dream
of azure welcomes
my unknown friends were preparing for me
and I would gaze at the plain of dawn
at the mossy roof of the bell-tower
snowed over with white storks.
Blond children
with wonderful amazement in their eyes
would open the posthumous
testaments of my songs.
(How many smiles I summoned
in my bitter loneliness
for the pleasure of people!)
Ah, the retinue that awaited
my entry to Jerusalem.
Like a silent Christ
I heard the trumpets of the heavens
foretold the streets
strewn with psalms
and patience did not fail me
in my burning agony.
But, my sister,
I no longer know

how to wait and to pray.
Listen, this evening
waving rosy veils
above the gardens
calls to my ancient sprit.
The twittering of birds
offends my seemly mourning.
My sister, be still;
cascades of warblings
do not bless my desolation.
I stay faithful in the arms
of your love.
I am no longer a poet
and I am afflicted.
Forgive me, my sister,
for this grief of mine
that lives outside your grief.

My sister,
a cloud always shadowed
your eyelids.
Leaning on the balcony
— even as a child —
you would gaze at the sea
unrolling in the dream
of endless solitude.
You would feed your heart
on the leaves of autumn.
The enigma of mother's shadow
was reflected in your eyes.
The pale light of your face
lingered on the floor
of our house.
We never saw you weep.
Only there on your temples
the delicate veins
patterns of azure light
signalled the fever of your sealed lips.
(How many times
when you were sleeping

I bent over them to read
your secret.)
Full of love and compassion
you would bind our wound
and be silent.
Your silence informed everything.
On winter evenings
you would walk alone in the woods
to nurse
naked sparrows,
to warm
frozen insects.
Drop by drop you gathered within you
the tears of the poor, of the humble.
And when our house fell
you remained upright and still
— shade of the Virgin —
to show me the stars
through the holes in the roof.
Now your silence has been broken
and in the small shell that you hid
I heard the cries of the ocean.
My sister, not a stone was left
for me to lean upon.

I still walk
in the wilderness of throngs
in unsuspecting streets.
No-one.
Children play without divining
bells that are ringing far away
stopping their blood.
People can still laugh,
I can still hear
talk that turns on other things
— merchant ships pass
near the lonely lighthouse
in the sea.
From the metopes of palaces
clocks sound:

nothing, nothing, nothing.
Some fall in love by chance,
some construct the event,
some keep books
telling of gaunt hermits.
Trains carry
fog and ghosts
out of deserted stations.
Lilacs shake
a dark blue remnant
of the faded dream
above stone foreheads.
Nothing.
And this faint scent
of childhood recollection
is consumed in vain
without echo.
Nobody sees.
Flakes of ash
cover the earth.
Oh God,
to shut my eyes
to cross my arms
and be carried off at the whim of the winds.
Thus profoundly tired
to roll in the abyss
while the speed of the fall
whistles in my ears
a song of rest.
Close the windows.
The light's impudence
blurs my tear.
Enough of flowery talk.
It does not serve.
Mother Silence
bring your hand
to my temples.
On my bare head
autumn woods
stir their shadows.
My sister, I am drowsy.

MY SISTER'S SONG

Where can I rest?
How can I sleep?
I have no bed.
And the sick dawn
finds the lamp of my vigil
burning once more.

— ◆ —

The evening hour
has come upon me far from you
my sister.
Venerable beauty
has tapped my shoulder
with a tender hand.
On the horizon dawns
the flame of a forgotten rose.
The gentle peaks
carry up
baskets of violets
to the transparent feet
of rest.
I hold in my smock
a newborn lamb
and I sink my spirit
in its soft eyes.
I gaze at the plains
quietly inhaling
the evening calm
and I greet the souls
of things.
Behind the flowering pear trees
your shadow
grieving watches me.
My sister, I have not forgotten you.
I fathom goodness
by your clemency.
I distribute smiles
on the lines and forms
illumined by your saintly light.
But while I gather you
a bunch of daisies

from the fields of evening,
you, my sister,
with frenzied eyes
like a flashing sword
light up the firmament,
but you do not know
that living things you see
reflected there
restore your image to yourself
through layers of silence and reverence.

My sister, I had promised
to bring you the immortal water.
I had promised to throw the sun
at your feet.
Now you cry out:
"My brother, I thirst;
where is the immortal water
that I may quench my thirst?
My brother, I am cold;
where is the sun
that I may warm my hands?"
And I stay motionless and helpless.
I who roamed
the heavens
cannot cover
one span of earth.
Beneath the snow I hear
the roots of our old garden
binding me to the ground.
And I have forgotten how to walk.
Filled with awe
I lean over the chaos
of your soul.
The stars collide
in the depths of your eyes
and the battles of the Gods
bleed our heart.
How to mould your burning
into a cool sculptured calm?

MY SISTER'S SONG

I had believed once in heaven,
but you have shown me
the depths of the sea
with its dead towns
its forgotten forests
its drowned voices.
And now heaven has plunged
— a wounded seagull —
into the sea.
My hand that built for you
a bridge over the abyss
has faltered.
Look at me
how naked and innocent
I lie down before you.
I am cold, my sister.
Who will bring us the sun
to warm our hands?
I listen, silent.
No-one is passing
on the night road.
The stars have foundered
in the corroded eyes
of the moulting eagle
that wavers on the edge
of dark battlements.
Your bound hands
block my way.
Only your voice wanders
the corridors of night
striking its long sword
on the tiles.
It is late.
Neither life nor death
receives me.
Where shall I go?

— ◆ —

My sister, I was mistaken.
I am not a god.
I do not determine anything.

Your fire vaporized
my power to quench it.
As you shook
light's golden dust
from the eyelashes of the universe
I gazed at the great crosses of mankind
standing on our evening horizon
and I love the sad people
who pass silent — white herds
marked on the forehead
with the red seal.
I read the history of the world
in a drop of your blood.
Ah, people, ah my brothers and sisters,
brothers and sisters of my sister,
in the infinite sea of your hearts
dreams founder in full sail,
the presumption of thoughts
and the indifferent musings of the Gods.
How many journeys have you made!
And you did not bring back with you
one image of growth
to adorn your empty houses,
one sea-shell
from those that the tempests
washed up on the land
— gleaming relic and trusty key —
to lock your doors
when the winds blow at night.
Your eyes remain forever
confined and guileless
— drops of rain coloured
with silence and doubt.
You have no refuge.
You die unresurrected
with no child's rosy lips
to say your name again
under the tranquil sky
of the new May.
But I,
I saw remembrance of you hover

— venerable dove
on my sister's shoulder.
My brothers and sisters
receive the apostate
on your broad bosom.
With tears I wash
your wounded feet.
With tears I cleanse my hands
of the dust of pride
that I may be worthy to caress your hair.

My sister,
come let us lean
like sick children
over the incorporeal garden
that has sunk within us
to heed
the dissolved fragrance
that has settled forgotten
on a dim corner of our hearts.
. . . On summer nights
enraptured we would see
the full moon rising
on the shore of our birthplace.
The silver road would carry us
to the azure murmurings of the universe.
Mother would be near
— a white angel
in the white nights.
We would hear her distant voice
and the soothing rustle of her gown
while our eyes were closing
in starry sleep.
Ah, sweet protection
that watched at our side
warming
the naked birds of our dreams.
Efflorescence of light enveloped us
and we fled, little sister,
between sky and sea.

... And then
the closed doors
the impassive windows
the backs turned.
Mother's voice dead.
Alone
hand in hand
in unknown towns
— two small suppliants
with our warm dream
under the flawed sky.
We no longer had shelter
or staff.
But we still knew how
to be loved
and to love.
Growing weary I would lean on you.
You would fix your gaze on mine
and you would bring me gold anemones
from your toil to my dream.
My sister,
approach once more and kiss
my burning brow.
Look,
I open for you the little skylight
and a slanting ray
outlines the shadow of your face.
Thrust off the night
and come to me
and we shall take each other, as then, by the hand
and wander through cold cities
— two small suppliants
with our old dream,
— two great princes
of love.

— ◆ —

Do you remember?
Mother once gave you
a pink dress
and a little pink parasol.

You would climb the flowering hillside
on a spring morning
ethereal and diaphanous
— a pink cloud of light.
You would gaze at the sky
as if something from above was calling you.
Only the sad plaits
of your black hair
lay heavy on your thin back.
I was afraid
that sometime you would disappear
with the rosy light
into the sunset.
Then I would gather
brighter shells
and many-coloured pebbles
on the shore of our island
to see your eyes
smiling
and bewitch your heart
that was quietly dissolving
in the grief of the world.
But you did not know how to laugh.
I would make wings of your tears
and go far away to bring you
the pollen of heaven
to absolve your silence.
But you did not know how to take.
You gave.
Only gave.
All your gifts
you shared out
and your hands
were left empty.
You bowed your head
— sorrowing bird —
in your dark wing
and sang the amazing song
of all the wounded world.
My sister,
raise your head.

I stoop beside you and bring you
our childhood dawns
that you may inhale
the saltness of our island,
the evening murmurings
and crossing the mist of homesickness
anchor beside me.
Return, my sister,
to little Bethlehem
that bore us beautiful and humble
and I, you will see, I will shed
dreams of Jerusalem
that took me far away from you
and I will stay forever at your side
— a modest cricket
to sing to you
on spring evenings.
Do you not hear me?

All was refused me,
I refused everything.
Nor does the thought console me.
Whatever I loved
death took from me
and madness.
I alone remained
beneath the ruins of my heaven
to count the dead.
The storm swept from my way
the pure footprints of God.
My beloved dead
have revived me
to weep for them.
And yet
the ruined mill
still turns its wings
above the reaped plains,
in the stillness
of the evening skies.
Ah, these wings

that touch my eyelids
with the languid movement
of pages read
and I follow
their strange command
without will and without oblivion.
Let them sleep at last
these wings that form
the tired gestures
of wounded birds
in the gloomy clouds
of eternal autumn.

How coldly sounds and colours
receive me this evening.
The sunset drags her golden greeting
on the shoulders of things.
What does this rosy light want?
Why this display
of insensible ceremony?
The trees and silence
have put on a pompous hue
of orators who speak
before blind statues.
Ah, how I hate
the soft clouds
that hang motionless flaming
in the complacent light.
Do they know me
my old friends?
No;
I need nothing.
It does not befit me to be pitied.
I bite my lips
and drink my blood.
I disdain
their dead beauty.
— Heaven, what are you boasting of?
I who am crushed
under your foot

will surpass your cold beauty
with my warm song.

— ◆ —

My sister,
only you were left me
to lean on your heart
and hear the pulse of men.
My life proceeded
beneath the canopy of your eyes.
You would come gentle and loving
in the evenings when bowed and silent
I wrote my angry verses
for the never-ending wars
of light and blood.
I felt your presence
behind the night.
The honeysuckle
of tender hours
covered my grey roof
when your footsteps were heard.
You would smile
and all of heaven would come
into my room.
Azure reflections
fluttered on the walls
and remembrance of our home
stirred my heart.
When I returned heavy
with night wanderings
and the proud bitterness of loneliness,
I would find the supper of love
steaming on the table
and childhood memory
— a frail butterfly —
would play around your lamp.
You would stay up
awaiting my return.
And when I,
the lover of Infinity,
would sink into the shadows

of nebulous doubts,
you
with your warm finger
would show me the footprints on the ground
and shape my ashes once again
into a human form.
I shared your stool
and so held
a place on earth.
I measured time
by your pulse.
I would listen for drops of coolness
somewhere near, falling
from a hidden well.
And the well dried.
You left.
You pulled heaven away
— blue dust
behind your footstep.
It is snowing.
Life, life,
you took from me
the last fleshly crumb.
I have no more tears.
I have no fear.
I have nothing else for them to take from me.
Poor, naked, and desolate —
here are my riches
that no one can
take from me.
I will not knock on any door.
I will not say any prayer.
Without bread
without rucksack
without bond
I take the road west
with long and steady strides
naked and entire,
worthy to touch God.

— ◆ —

A whitish cloud
of the watchful moon
slowly dissolves
in the blueness of dawn.
The window panes on the sea-front
— a procession of tearful eyes —
give back
in ghastly duplication
the pale sinking of the moon.
Ah, these wanings
that cast doubt equally
on both night
and day
and hover imponderable.
Below,
the grey sea
reflects the sky-hued tremor
that lingers
on the frail backs
of seagulls.
Shadowy masts
line the horizon
motionless
in readiness for motion.
For a new journey?
For a new return?
The mist delays
the confirmation of the sun.
Nothing is ever repeated.
Profit
and loss
leave their traces
on the whitish moon
that slowly vanishes
in the dawn.
The seagulls come from far away,
they greet
the moored boats,
they circle
— a cluster of lilies —
the rusted anchors.

My sister,
your shore is receding.
The journey of discovery is beginning.
A glimmer of light is traced
on the half-open eyelid
of sky and sea.

— ◆ —

My sister
a bright line
is drawn around
our closed door.
Revival floods
the stale air
with sea noises.
A may-beetle pesters
the closed window panes.
The sun pours
into the room's disorder
and its inadmissible shudder
possesses us.
What hand of blessing
drew its shadow
on the cold walls?
Here is the trophy of life
above genuflections.
Here is the flag of spring
above tombs.
The shrivelled sheets
rise up
— sails on ships.
The bed moves.
A breath.
Absorbing dilation.
I obey the command
I open my arms and accept
the irresistible.
The lovely faces
of women parade
their bright procession
on my flesh.

Suspended, the morning swallows
draw the hands of mist away
from my forehead.
I can weep no more.
Song has conquered me.
Song has given me victory.

The sun, the sun
melting the frozen landscape
in my eyes.
Vigorous song raised up
on the scaffolding of heaven
builds with bare arms
my home.
Light ripples
in the muscles of my voice.
I hear the chain links
falling and breaking.
I hear the white horsemen
passing outside singing
war marches.
The windows have opened wide
above the morning sea.
My doorstep brightens
like an open eye.
My sister,
I can stay no more.
My absence will bring you
the immortal water.
And I who could not
save you from life
will save you from death.
There are the roads
brilliant and clear in the sunshine.
Stand aside, my sister,
that I may pass by your bound hands.
I have hung on my breast
the talisman you sewed me
one spring evening — do you remember? —
when we were very young.

MY SISTER'S SONG

In it is a little red earth
to recall our last home,
a dried rose-leaf
from the garden of our house
and a little dust from the wall
that we scraped one night with our nails
for the final long exile.
Goodbye, my sister.
Kiss for me the sparrows in our yard
the innocent children
the sad mothers
who embroider by the lamp
and the young who build
unsuspecting and determined
their place
on the borders of life and death.

Now I give myself back to the world.
Fair nature
with a broad fan
from the boughs of palm-trees
refreshes my limbs
and dissolves my tears.
The recovered taste
for age-long health
sings on my palate
and smarts my gums
like unripe fruits.
I gaze at heaven
throwing amicably onto the earth
a handful of seed.
My sister,
beyond you and me,
beyond our dim gaze
beyond the dim line of earth
there at the root of all
listen to the wave of impulse
which supreme, uncontrollable and inexplicable
created us and governs us.
What can we say?

I open the gates
with terrified wonder
in front of Creation
and change the pain into ecstasy
and the cry into prayer.
The bright tresses of horizons
wipe
my bleeding feet
and I climb light and happy
towards the summit of the smile.
Sun, sun,
father, my protector,
receive me now.
No ring binds
my wings to the earth.
The light shines bright, higher
than your love, my sister,
higher than my love . . .

— ◆ —

*The calm face
of eternity shatters the distorted mirrors
of tears and yet we have within us still
a very storm of tears.*

——— ◆ ———

The march of the ocean

Night harbour
lights drowned in the water
faces without memory or coherence
illumined by the passing lights of distant ships
then sunk in the shadows of the journey
slanting sails hung with dream lamps
like the broken wings of angels who have erred
soldiers with helmets
between night and the charcoal fire
wounded hands like the pardon that came too late.

Captives bound to the anchors
a chin around the horizon's neck
and other chains on children's feet
and on the hands of dawn that hold a daisy.

And the masts persist
in counting the stars
with the help of quiet recollection
— a bouquet of seagulls in the dawn calm.

Colour leaves the face of day
and the light cannot find a statue
to enter, to be glorified and made calm.

Shall we still protect then
the sun's open wound
that wells up with flower seeds
on the same march
on the same quest
in the fertile veins of spring
when swallows resume their wheeling

tracing an amorous nought
on the unconquered firmament?

What wound
has not yet been granted us
to make complete
the divinity of the god?

— ◆ —

We had our garden at the sea's edge.
The sky slipped in through the windows
while mother sitting
on the low stool
embroidered the spring fields
with open doorways in white houses
with dreams of storks on the thatched roof
drawn against clear pale blue.

You had not yet come.
I would look to the west and see you
— a rosy sheen in your hair
— a shadowy smile deep in the sea.

Mother held my hands.
But I
behind her tender shoulder
behind her pale hair
smoothed with an aroma of patience and nobility
would gravely look at the sea.

There in the blue curve of the mountains
a seagull would call me
in the depths of the evening.

— ◆ —

The mirror shattered that sketched
the dawn and the garden.

THE MARCH OF THE OCEAN

With the sad flutes of flowers
we buried the first swallow
the day before yesterday.

Then the children sat alone
at the evening window
to see the dying sun.

Behind the white yard-wall
the road was waking
and as the light faded golden far off
the great shadow of the mountains climbed
with death's silent footstep
to our white hands
to our hearts
to our bowed foreheads.

Mother, who is ringing
the azure bell of the horizon?

— ◆ —

Silver cloud beside the moon.

Old seamen who no longer have boats
who no longer have nets
sit on the rock
and smoking their pipes
muse on journeys and regrets and the shadow.

But we know nothing
about the ashes in the taste of the journey.
We know the journey and the pale blue
half-circle of the horizon
like the sea god's fierce eyebrow.

We jump into the boats
we loosen the ropes
and we sing the sea

gazing at the silver cloud
beside a spring moon.

What jewelled town
sleeps behind the mountains?
What lights tremble beyond in the night
calling to us?

— ◆ —

There are small white graves
of innocent seagulls
far away on unknown deserted islands
that knew only
light from the benighted ocean.
There we placed our first flowers
our first sob the first thought.

We heard the song of the sea
and we can sleep no more.

Mother
do not hold my hand.

— ◆ —

The sea the sea
in our minds our souls and our veins the sea.

We saw ships bearing mythical countries
here on the golden sand
where evening wayfarers linger.
We dressed our childhood loves
in moist seaweed.
We offered the gods of the shore
bright shells and pebbles.

Morning colours dissolved in the water
sunset's fire on the shoulders of seagulls
masts that point to infinity
open doorways at nightfall

and above our stoney sleep
hovering resplendent undying
the song of the sea
comes through the little windows
sketching gardens and dreams radiant
on the damp panes and sleeping foreheads.

— ♦ —

Anguished and sleepless rhythm.
Out on the barren rocks
we homeless barefoot children
behold Beauty there
walking with naked feet in the sea
we hear her voice
that quivers with serene echoes
with the phosphorescence of the stars
that plant golden stories
in the green depths.

Venerable heart
unsuspecting child's heart
that you never deny.

We stretched our hands
to gather flowers from the stars
to gather stars from our hearbeats
that answered the sea crying to us
to hold on to Beauty's robe
travelling towards infinity
by the road the huge summer moon
sketched on the open sea.

— ♦ —

Naked we wrestled on the sand at midday
with the wet bodies of twelve-year-old children
more often for the embrace than for the struggle
more often for the struggle than the victory
the victory alone.

Salt hair
sunburned thighs

the sighing wave in the kiss
the sea beyond the spasm.

Middays descended roaring in whirlwinds of fire
to wind the fishermen's houses round with white flames
to burn the hearts that didn't resist.

Outside the windows the gentle strumming sea-breeze
the luminous face of calm
in summer's white memory
with a dark blue shadowy beam
aslant on its downy cheek.

Golden breath of endless water
nets basking on the rocks
boats filled with fruits and flowers
and there are our houses
our houses sketched on the sea.

— ◆ —

Beckoning from the shore
the red stones
the small lilac flowers
and the girls.

Who is calling us
from the terrace of our house?

We built our house in the sea.
There are pearls in the shells
and great coral woods in the lonely depths.

We made our flute
with the bones cast up yesterday evening
at our yard by the tempest singing.

Listen to our song mother
the new journey's song.

You who weep over death
do not know us.

THE MARCH OF THE OCEAN

The sea does not lament.
It sings.

— ◆ —

Released from Sunday service.
Whitewashed yard
facing the sea the silent bell tower
that sounded All Souls' Day for sailors
and now laughs in the sunshine.

— ◆ —

We have our father's pipes in our mouths
beneath our school caps.
On our breasts the southern cross embroidered
and the ancient mermaid.

Dark sailor vest
closed to the neck
when the girls see us
we assume the rolling gait
of world-travelled captains.

There trembles in the glances of young girls
the sound of a great morning forest
a clear sure music.

But while the tranquil houses
greet us tenderly
with musk plant drooping on the white wall
there will come in again among us
to conquer us once more
the radiant light from the great ocean.

You there captain
eat your dry bread quickly
and the black olive
steeped in salt and sun
on top of the sheer rock.

Time to set sail.

— ◆ —

As we draw breath
the zephyr's pale blue sail swells
its luminous folds billowing
as they vanish behind the serene breasts
of the distant mountains.

Our hearts that loved the sea
have no boundaries.

Health's unfaltering pennant
driven into the rock
greets the sky
waving above men
great cooling shadows
from the morning sea
with white sails and islands
in mid-May's full bloom.

— ◆ —

The silver moon reflecting
creeps solitary behind the rocks.

On childhood's pillow polished shells
in sleep blue ocean voices
the Sirens with their fishbone lyres.

Ah Goddess of the distant island
stalactites in your sea cavern
even if they chant the sleep of pale serenity
even if your bright breast vies with
the dark blue circle of the starlit sea
and there is a gold garland of bees
around the fountain where the light faintly penetrates
perfuming the shade of the enormous trees —
you know the cunning one will leave.

Laertes with his hound
will wait in vain on the rock.

As He came out of the sea
golden from the dawn water
his pubes sketched in the sun's frame
Nausicaa fled with the lovely terrified virgins
behind the trees
their bare feet fluttering in the air
like a multitude of doves
white light reflected on the green verdure.

. . . Out on the terrace beside the sea
our frugal evening table.
Spring dipped the wheaten bread in wine
and the moon secretly painted
on Greek earthenware pitchers
scenes from Troy.

You knew we would go mother
and you salted our supper with a tear
bowed and sad beneath the stars
and the girls sighed on the island window sills
who were betrothed to Odysseus.

Blood we spent and seed
with kites and clouds
above the clear waters
with small wooden caïques
in blue bays
smelling sweetly of farewells
with kisses beside the boats at the old breakwater
behind the ruined summer windmill
preparing the great journey to the unknown.

And when we returned at evening
with bleeding hands and fractured knees
bringing the spoils of weariness:
watery icons that deny form
rose-coloured evening chimes
the spasm's remorse
the emptiness of the contest —
there beneath the shadow of the cemetery by the sea

our childhood eyes perceived the silence
we heard the night's coming
heard the flute of beauty
that consoles the saddened brow
and justifies our fate.

Who shatters God's soul
and our joy
who divides the silence
into thousands of names and stars
that moving illumine our hands
and trace circles of solitude
on the same sea
that preserve the fire of creation
but do not rest?

— ◆ —

Sea birds hovering
by silent rock caves
sketches of angels
embroidered with stars at the water's fretted edge
near the resisting pebbles
in the green shade of the breakwater
beneath the wondering eyes
of pensive boys.

— ◆ —

The wound of departing day
writing in blood horizons and rememberance
drew the God's imperfection
the gesture the dream the creation.

Serene knowledge
in children's wide eyes
on the serious lips of adolsecents
who did not count the shipwrecked
knowledge that glorifies
the stars coming out
from the open wound of God
to soothe
the wound of man.

THE MARCH OF THE OCEAN

We closed our eyes
in our white ancestral bed.

The lamp put out.
Framed in the window
the sea secretly glimmering.
Behind hedges and trees
we heard
its loud voice calling us
filling our sleep with an azure landscape
flowering with snow-white sails
with gardens of seagulls that mused voiceless
perched on the stone brink of the unknown
above the dark magnetic chasm.

From there God's cry named us.
Tomorrow we will swim again
tomorrow we will journey again
tomorrow the dawn will ask our endurance
and we will answer to the sea.

We wrote the first line on the sand
while the patient masts watched us sternly
and the wave whispered everlasting homesickness.

We stayed on the rock as if carved in flight
and gazed at moons writing circles
asking about our secret
about ships carrying white ghosts
about the journey that doesn't end
about the anchor that doesn't hold in the water.
We touched our wound and time
and we escaped.

The journey is always with us
and the ceaseless roar of the sea.

The ships had come at dawn

laden with wheat and coal and wine
for dreaming captains
for fuel for the fire.

You threw away the bread the wine and the coal
and stayed naked in the sea
without a cloth to cover your ribs
or love to hide your eyes.

The hour was coloured like the secret pearl
of dawn's deep meditation
its distant voice filled with danger and promise.
You looked at your body in the water
and loved the water forgetting your body.

Ah, journey without cargo
fire without coal
hunger without bread
thirst and rapture without wine.

Now it is too late to go back.

If the wave is warmer than love
and the ship warmer than the port
you yourself know it
flight singing in your hair
as you face the horizon with the sea horn
sounding endless migration.

The ships went away and left us
without bread wine or coal
in the very middle of the sea.

— ◆ —

All night we wept
bent over a seagull's white bier.

Mother's lamp shone from our fireside
a delicate branch of light
in the Virgin's transparent palm.

THE MARCH OF THE OCEAN

Heavy sleep at daybreak
in the story of shells
candles melted
in the church by the sea.

And it was the ship waiting
with prow carved in the dawn light
sword of the wind.

Sleep this evening with heart bitter
as fishermen's bread in the storm.

Tomorrow we'll uproot the crosses
in the cemetery by the sea
and make children's boats
and carve on tombstones
little statues of beauty and the sea
to fill the desolate house
to entice life and ourselves
despite the god of denial
beneath the god who blesses.

The masts lost
the smoke sunk
behind the silent curve of water
like the knee of a mother sleeping
and the sleepless journey in our breasts
sleepless as the wind and the sea
in a winter evening.

Soft hills travel in the mist
and the sick sun drowses
on the damp stones of evening.

Cranes on high
triangle of regret.

A small missal of solitude
in the evening rain
the iconostasis of Saint Nicholas on the shore

where autumn stops
to throw a coin of bitter sorrow and yellow leaf
while the roar of the tempest fades on the darkened sand
under the tearful starlight of a silent September.

Gather blue marbles
from childhood days of toys and crying
so that you may carve the ocean's statue
staining your hands with blood on cloudy afternoons
when the sea's pale reflection
draws a circle of luminous remorse
high in the vacant air.

— ◆ —

In the small green house on the shore
winter overtook us all alone.

The balconies deserted
and on the pallid shore
the mist steps noiselessly.

Decaying yellow leaves
silent death of chrysales
seaweed blocking roads and doors
memory wooded with cypress trees.

At the road's turning the shadow of silence.

From the windows we saw the last
summer visitors leaving
and the little caïque its baskets empty.

Ships sleep in the port
and the wind's grey flags
rattle on bare masts.

Shortly will come
the grieving rain
to wash away the lyrical names
the childhood drawings

and the glimmer of the sea
from summer boats.

In a flash of lightning
we will read fate
in our open palms
and will not have
one word to feed solitude
or two crumbs of bread
to feed the few sparrows
dying on the lonely road.

The trees on the quayside
bowed and forlorn
— wooden husks of summer
in the ransacked dusk.

Where did the orchestra of little girls go
in the seaside garden
there where the sailors drank in the evening
among the trees
and dancing leapt in the air
for the moon's gold coin reflected
in the girls' hair behind the basil plants?

At nights
only the sea's huge green reflection
wanders desolate on the steep rocks.

Silent we pass through
dark rooms
before dim mirrors
that no longer know us
and we hear the footsteps of silence
the wind and the sea
on our drowsy senses.

Something from the safety of the void —
a locked door in the evening
or a procession of cypress trees sketched

in autumn starlight's silver vagueness.

And when the lonely full moon
rains patience and oblivion
we open the window
and pray.

We thank you God
for leaving us thus alone thus grieving
so that we can gaze without awe at heaven
and be serene and boundless like infinity
forgotten and unknown like the unknown.

— ♦ —

Night. I stand in the dark doorway
the invisible mountain range in the distance
and call the god's name
in the snowstorm of stars
in the transparent shadow where men
sleep and die
in the solitude that returns my voice
in a thousand voices.

— ♦ —

Where did they all go leaving me here
to gaze at my empty palms
to keep company with silence and rain?

Sorrowful unto death
I see the empty sky
and welcome a large cloud
and I am like a grieving lamb
abandoned and alone
in the middle of a dark valley.

Oh God, why have they all gone from me?

Beneath my torn clothes
I have a tender heart
of birds and flowers.
(How many nights did I cry in secret

for a butterfly's wound.)

Let it all go. Let everything go.
I will stay once more
facing the broad sky
facing the wide sea
to sing
without bitterness or complaint.
Let everything go.
As I remain alone
so I come nearer to men
and so I am nearer to God.

I hear my voice
abandoned in the wind
and I warm my days.

A childhood chorus
follows the evening
disrobing the silence
reviving the spring.

But mother I am still cold.

Evening has fallen already.
The last autumn crickets
whittle the shadows in hedges
with small trusting voices.
Search in your heart
for the sun that has left.

And as twilight lengthens
into our souls will drip
the scent from a rose
a drop of dew on the eyelids
the last evening light
on two naked hands crossed
on a face marbled
by the silver arc of the sea.

— ◆ —

They took the sea's song from us
they bound our sea feet.

Silent and wondering children
with salted eyelashes
with wide blue eyes
fearful we pass through the large towns
beneath hospitals that smell of sleep and sweat
beneath houses with red lamps
beneath large buildings
emitting blood night and plunder.

Mother mother
we denied
your tears' tender wisdom.
Where is your forgiving hand
with its patient endurance
where is your hand
that we may hear the dawn and the sea
and warm our solitude?

Mother
heaven has perished
in the tears of the innocent.

We who walked at nights
in woods white as pearls
we who carved in stone
the dream's serene form
do not know how to walk
on roads that every day are stained
with fair Jesus' blood.

Behind the walls they lie in wait for us.
Flocks of wood pigeons
are startled out of corners.

Doors gape in the night.
Swords flash.

A decapitated moon.

With human bones
men prepare stairways
to climb up.

Lord, Lord
and we here
in the middle of great roads
awkward and sad
with empty satchel in our hands
with a nightingale's cage on our back
with remembrance of the wide sea on our brow
with innocent and wondering hands that do not beg.

Mother nothing is left to us.
Where shall we shelter?
Where shall we sleep?

There where hands and houses empty
the sea takes her prime place
in night's back rooms.
Dark panoplies
plaster masks
love's honied smile
portraits of growing children
no longer hang on the walls.

Rippling alone there
proud cold inexhaustible and free
the glimmering ocean.

Brown-skinned child with blue eyes
thick hair combed by the sea
child whose carefree step never questioned the earth
proud child who refused Sunday church
you made kites and boats with exercise books
do you remember the old captain
who forgot the harbour gazing at the stars

singing the sea to win back his youth?

And so at the hour
night's last smile left us
and we had no other ship to embark on
and the quays were without lights or passengers
we encountered our shadow ah child of the sea
we encountered you with a spring moon in your hands
walking alone on the shore among rocks
where seals and crabs serenely dream.

— ◆ —

Eyes sated with pictures of water
and craving still for water
stars parading in sleeping seagulls' memories
sudden onslaught of dolphins panic of sea creatures
and on the water's broken mirrors
the galaxy's cyclic flight.

Frightened silence leaves once more
for the distant sleeping shore
— the fair daughter of drowned captains
lives in the ruins of the ancient breakwater
and every night when the moon is full
drunken sailors pursue her.

Lord of the sky the earth and the sea
until when shall we watch and wait
until when shall we thirst
until when shall we not die?

— ◆ —

To reach where the light halted
shattering into wounds and roses
that would silence the wheeling
of weary swallows
you should have toiled
to the last rung of dusk
your breathing shortened unto death.

On broken evenings

when lamps in houses wept
when children prayed
at the sick Virgin's bed
in the snow where a large
lonely moon was dying
in the wind that crucified
the amorous feathers of birds
we gathered warmth and light
to make blossom a hymn of spring.

Yet victory did not come, did not end.

And so alone are we
that death is in love with us
and our shadow walks on the white shore
like a peaceful ocean bird
sated with radiance and calm
spent by night and love.

Yet the hour before dawn did not come.

Who will now bring us
exiled ships returning
laden with dawns and doves
childhood smiles and tears?
Who will bring back to us
the great company of stars
that foundered in our shining eyes?

Lord, Lord,
bring me again
prayer's heavenly gown
bring me the heart
that ignores the rain
and blossoms with swallows
bring me migrations and returns
that I may be able to weep
for a firefly's wound
that I may be able to sin
and repent

when our island bell
sounds above the sea
Sunday's pure innocence
our own lost innocence
our lost health.

In birds' gentle eyes
a vision of plains will remain
with their scarlet poppies
and golden abundance of corn.

In little windows by the shore
loves and geraniums will flower again
and a Christ child will come to take our hand
and play until evening under the lilacs
with storks sea-breezes and sun.

And when night falls we will jump into white caïques
and with the nets of sorrowing Biblical fishermen
we will catch the watery moon
and lie quietly with her
brightening our sleep with silent angels
who have not yet learned to laugh and to cry
but only to smile in the dream
of unborn Creation.

Islands with trees quiet in the peaceful evening
the doves of peace are silent there
there we are silent gathering the roses of day
while the evening shadow falls on the white page
where we trace out life beside the shore.

We will not read what we have written.
We will raise our eyes
waiting for the cascading galaxy
behind an almond tree of white cloud
that lingers above the sea.

The season comes again
that knows neither time nor regret.

Serene sound of assuaged water
the light footsteps of fishermen on the sand
the children are asleep in boats
and angels bathe in their dreams.

Smell of grass and aroma of stars.
Mountain ranges dissolve far off in the opal sky.

Our weary hands
sprinkled with fresh dew
and our hair perfumed
with the shadow of yesterday's grief.

Mother the world is boundless.

The great harp of twilight
left in the densely shaded wood.
A rosy cloud takes fire
in the sunset's conflagration.

God hold this colour fast
that we may know our mind
that is defeated but does not submit.

We still need
this distant sympathy
that suffers for what is spoiled
preserving the dream
of incorruption.

Evening passes by
on the deserted shore
the jar of ashes
on her bare shoulder.

On her thoughtful face a smile has dawned
that nourishes our quest that nourishes our vigil
impelling the glorious oracle
of our fate.

— ◆ —

This evening the universe breathes the scent
of the watchful god's seed.
We water the roots
in the eternal fountain
that springs from the depths of night
and fills the skulls of the dead with roses.

Turn on the lights on distant wharfs
embroider with stars the sleeping sea
raise the plundered lands.

Here silence assumes a voice.
Here lives forever all that has gone.
Here is no flight and no decay.

Evening song above the seas
accompanied by the absence of things
that bloom in the eternal cycle
of silence and of love.

The sea gazes at her own face
in the sea.

— ◆ —

Take subdued ideals
take the knowledge that shrivelled our youthful senses.

Take the unfruitful calm
that remains wearied on the rock
building her temple and her tomb
with the wood from our ancient ships.

Leave us only
night's rapture
when mothers await
at the flowering door
their strange untameable children
who missed their evening meal
who naked swim all day

who look for seagulls' nests
and all night utter in their sleep
words we do not know
about ships and clouds and Angels
about certain mad Angels who live
in reefs of coral crimson
about certain fair Angels
who are betrothed to the sea
and forgetting God
play frenzied trumpets
made with the bones
of shipwrecked poets.

Leave us only
night's rapture
when children fish for stars
in snow-white caïques
when adolescents naked and beautiful
look beauty in the eyes
without distrust or fear.

Give us back
the paper boats
that we may anchor
at the familiar port
of our first home.

For a moment
we will kneel on the sand
and we will pray
before our unkneeling shadow
while the sad Virgin of the sea
will quietly open the church door
and will come and kiss our hair
damp with the fine dew of the stars
the silence and the night.

But we will refuse again
love's kiss
that soothes and binds.

Unknown in the unknown
beautiful and unsubdued
we will travel forever
in the silvery forests of the moon
in the lonely islands of the stars
without knowing God
without finding God
like the pulsation of divinity
that in creating destroys itself.

— ◆ —

Night harbour
lights drowned in the water
faces without memory or coherence
illumined in succession
by the passing lights
of distant ships
and then sunk
in the shadow of the eternal journey
sails hung with dream lamps
and slanting
like the broken wings
of angels who have erred
soldiers with helmets
between night and the charcoal fire
hands wounded
like the pardon that came too late.

A great fire on the peak
burning the shadow's heart.

Captives bound to the anchors
in the red glare
a chain
tight on the horizon's neck
and round the hands of dawn
that hold a daisy.

Colour leaves the face of day
and the light cannot find a statue
to enter, to be glorified and made calm.

THE MARCH OF THE OCEAN

Brothers and sisters
how can I stay far from you?

— ◆ —

The sea, the sea
books do not answer the question
the question does not heal the wound.
From our wound the sea begins.

Dreams of the journey
at the last curve of tears.

Who banishes the sun
from children's hair
from our great heart?

Hoist the sails
weigh the anchor.
Forward and the old port slips away
forward and the dawn gleams
with all the tears of our ancestors.

A chain does not befit the sea's ankles
a chain does not befit our sea heart.

Goodbye to loves and countries.

Seabirds in the light and in the brine
we dream of journeys, in full sail
our ears unsealed to the Sirens' voices
our eyes watchful.
There is neither smoke nor Ithaca.
No other horizons now beyond the horizon.

The eternal song of the sea answers the void
and fills its emptiness with heart and with sun.

— ◆ —

Ah, stormy nights
fresh winds lashing

foam on window panes
smoking lamps in fishermen's houses
the fears of sorrowing girls
mending socks for the exiled
vigilant beacons with the eyes of mothers
and the sea unpitying and boundless
like the mind of God
possessed tender and untamed
like the hearts of poets.

Ghosts of shipwrecked captains
their pipes still in their mouths
riding on flashes of lightning
sunken ships returning
to night harbours
lost crews
standing outside closed doors
wait
seeking dumbly for their lives
holding tropical pictures
azure plains with enormous lilies
and naked ebony women.

These bewail unseeing.

But we
who talked for hours with the sea
we who have always on our lips
the fresh strong new
taste of the journey
accept the eternal gifts of death.

And when mothers
curse the sea
and old captains
pace restlessly
in closed rooms
we
open the doors
run to the high rocks
and raise our cry

THE MARCH OF THE OCEAN

in the night
leaving the storm behind
forgetting bread and hearth
cooling our fevered brow
with the wide sea's rage.

Sea, sea
as with you
so with us
we will not succumb to the night
and to sleep.

We will not deign to cry out:
we have won the victory for ever.

— ◆ —

Joy of tempest
of calm
of departure
joy of the eternal journey
let the lights on the shore blow out
that we may enter the ocean's heart
the inexhaustible psalm of the night waves
while God
from the height of his vast solitude
casts stones at our boldness
with bright dreams.

Ah endless pain ah world-wide joy
universal fire
that burns the night's black hair
lights up the dawn above white sails
above high masts
where poets climb
to hail the new face of God
mirrored smiling in the water
framed by two ecstatic seagulls.

Sun, sun
that dyes the sea with blood
naked I offer myself to your flame

to light the eyes of men.

My brothers and sisters
listen to your voice, my voice
listen to the song of the sun and the sea.

———◆———

The Moonlight Sonata

A spring evening. A large room in an old house. An elderly woman, dressed in black, speaks to a young man. They haven't turned on the light. A pitiless moonlight comes in through the windows. I should mention that the woman in black has published two or three interesting, religiously inspired collections of poetry. The woman in black now speaks to the young man.

>Let me come with you. What a moon tonight!
>It is kind, the moon — my hair
>will not be white. The moon
>will turn it golden once again. You won't see the white.
>Let me come with you.
>
>When there is a moon, shadows lengthen in the house,
>invisible hands draw the curtains,
>a pallid finger writes forgotten words
>on the dusty piano — I don't want to hear them. Be quiet.
>
>Let me come with you
>a little further down, to the brickyard wall,
>to where the road turns and the cement town
>appears, ethereal, whitewashed with moonlight,
>so unconcerned and incorporeal,
>so real like metaphysics
>you can believe at last that you exist and do not exist
>that you never existed, time and decay do not exist.
>Let me come with you.
>
>We shall sit for a while on the low stone wall up on the hill,
>and as the spring wind blows on us
>we can then imagine we are flying away
>because, many times, even now, I hear the noise of my gown

like the noise of two strong wings opening and closing,
and when you are wrapped in this sound of flight
you feel your neck taut, your ribs, your flesh;
and held thus firm in the muscles of the azure air,
in the strong nerves of height,
you are not concerned whether you are going or coming
nor does it matter that your hair has turned white,
(this does not grieve me — what grieves me
is that my heart too has not turned white).
Let me come with you.

I know that each of us walks alone in love,
alone in glory and in death.
I know it. I've tried it. It's not enough.
Let me come with you.

This house is haunted, it's driving me away —
I mean it's worn out, the nails are springing out,
the pictures throw themselves down as if plunging into the void,
the plaster falls silently
like a dead man's hat falling from the hook in the dark corridor,
like a frayed woollen glove falling
from the knee of silence
or like a strip of moonlight falling on the old,
disembowelled armchair.

Once it too was young — not the photo you are gazing at with such disbelief —
I'm talking about the armchair, very comfortable, you could sit in it for hours on end
and with your eyes closed dream about anything at all —
a smooth, sandy beach, wet, glossed by the moon,
more glossy than my old patent leather shoes that I bring each month to the shoe-
shine parlour at the corner,
or the sail of a fishing boat disappearing far off, rocked by its own breath,
its triangular sail like a handkerchief folded in two only, on the bias
as if having nothing to enfold or to hold,
not waving wide open in farewell. I've always had a passion for handkerchiefs,
not to keep anything tied,
flower seeds or camomile gathered in the fields at sunset,
or to tie them in four knots like the caps the workers wear
on the building site opposite

or to wipe my eyes. My eyesight is still good.
I've never worn glasses. Handkerchiefs were just a fancy of mine.

Now I fold them in four, eight, sixteen
to occupy my fingers. And now I remember
I would count the music like this when I went to the Odeon
in a blue pinafore and white collar, with two blond plaits —
eight, sixteen, thirty-two, sixty-four —
hand in hand with my little peach-tree of a friend, all light and pink blossom,
(pardon these words — a bad habit) — thirty-two, sixty-four — and my family
had great hopes for my musical talent. However, I was talking about the armchair —
disembowelled — the rusty springs are showing, the straw —
I thought I'd take it to the upholsterer's nearby
but where is the time, the money, the will — how would you begin to repair it? —
I thought of throwing a sheet over it — I was afraid
of the white sheet in such a moonlight. Here sat people
who dreamed great dreams just as you and I do,
and now they are resting beneath the earth untroubled by the rain or by the moon.
Let me come with you.

We shall stand for a while at the top of the marble stair of Saint Nicholas,
then you will go down and I shall come back
with my left side warm from a chance touch of your jacket
and square lights shining still from small neighbourhood windows
and this snow-white mist from the moon like a great procession of silver swans —
and I do not regret this phrase, because I
have conversed on many spring nights in the past with God who appeared to me
clothed in the hazy glory of such a moonlight,
and to Him I sacrificed many young men, more beautiful even than you.
Thus pure and untouchable I dissolved in my pure white flame in the white moonlight,
consumed by the voracious eyes of men and the hesitant rapture of adolescents,
besieged by superb sun-tanned bodies,
strong limbs (that I pretended not to see) exercised in swimming, in rowing, in the
        stadium, in football,
foreheads, lips, and necks, knees, fingers, and eyes,
breasts and arms and thighs (that I really didn't see) —
you know, sometimes, in admiring, you forget what you are admiring, your
        admiration is enough —
God what glowing eyes, exalting me to the denying stars
because, thus besieged from without and within,

no other road was left me except only upwards or downwards. — No, it's not enough.
Let me come with you.

I know it's late. Let me,
because for so many years, days and nights and purple mid-days, I was alone,
resolute, alone, and chaste,
even in my marriage bed chaste and alone,
writing glorious verses at God's knee,
verses which, I assure you, will remain as if engraved on faultless marble
beyond my life and your life, far beyond. It's not enough.
Let me come with you.

This house can no longer endure me.
I cannot bear to carry it on my back.
You always have to take care, take care,
to prop up the wall with the big sideboard
to prop up the sideboard with the carved antique table
to prop up the table with the chairs
to prop up the chairs with your hands
to put your shoulder under the hanging beam.
And the piano, like a black coffin, closed. You don't dare to open it.
Taking care all the time lest they fall, lest you fall, I cannot bear it.
Let me come with you.

This house in spite of all its dead, does not intend to die.
It insists on living with its dead
on living on its dead
on living on the certainty of its own death.
With worn-out beds and shelves it still provides for its dead.
Let me come with you.

Here, however quietly I move about in the evening mist,
either in slippers or barefoot,
something will creak: a pane cracks or a mirror,
I hear footsteps — they are not mine.
Outside, in the street these footsteps may not be heard —
regret, they say, wears wooden shoes —
and if you go to look in this or that mirror,
behind the dust and the cracks,
you can make out your face more dimmed and torn.

THE MOONLIGHT SONATA

Your face — you asked nothing else in life but to keep it clear and whole.
The rim of the glass gleams in the moonlight
like a round razor — how can I take it to my lips?
However thirsty I am, how can I take it? Do you see?
I am still inclined to similes . . .   this at least remains,
this assures me still that I exist.
Let me come with you.

Sometimes at the evening hour I think I hear
the bear keeper passing outside the windows with his lumbering old bear
her fur all thorns and thistles
raising dust on the neighbourhood street
a solitary cloud of dust, smoke of incense in the twilight
after the children have gone home for supper and are not allowed out any more
although they can sense behind the walls the old bear's step.
The tired bear walks on in the knowledge of her loneliness, not knowing where
        or why —
she is heavy now, and can no longer dance on her hind legs or wear her lace cap to
        amuse the children, the idlers, the exacting,
and all she wants to do is to lie on the ground
letting them step on her belly, so playing her last game,
showing her fearsome strength in resignation,
her indifference to the interests of others, the rings on her lips, her hunger,
her indifference to pain and life
and its certain ally death — even if death is slow to come —
her final indifference to death as if she knew of a life of struggle
in knowledge and deed above her slavery.

But who can play that game to the end?
The bear rises again and walks on
submitting to her strap, her rings, her hunger,
smiling with torn lips at the five and ten piece coins the beautiful and unsuspecting
        children throw to her
(beautiful precisely because they are unsuspecting)
and saying thank you. Because the only thing that bears grown old
have learned to say is: thank you, thank you.
Let me come with you.

This house is drowning me. Even the kitchen
is like the bottom of the sea. The hanging coffee pots glow

like the big round eyes of improbable fish,
the plates gently quiver like jellyfish,
sea-weed and shells catch onto my hair — and I can't unravel them.
I can't rise again to the surface —
the tray falls soundless from my hands — I swoon
and see the bubbles from my breath rising, rising.
I try to divert myself by gazing at them
and wonder what anyone above seeing these bubbles would think —
someone drowning or a diver searching the depths?

And indeed not a few times have I found there, in the depths of drowning,
corals and pearls and treasures from wrecked ships,
unexpected encounters, past, present, and future,
a confirmation almost of eternity,
a respite, a smile of immortality, as they say,
a touch of happiness, a thrill, rapture even,
corals and pearls and sapphires;
only I don't know how to give them — no, I'll give them;
only I don't know who would take them — I'll give them anyway.
Let me come with you.

One moment until I get my jacket.
We must beware of this weather, changeable as it is.
There is damp in the evenings, and the moon
don't you think it increases the dampness?

Let me button your shirt — how strong your chest is, —
what a strong moon — the armchair, I tell you — and when I lift the cup from the table
there remains beneath a hole of silence, quickly I put my hand over it
so as not to look in — I leave the cup back in its place;
and the moon a hole in the world's skull — don't look in,
it is a strong magnet pulling you — don't look, don't look,
listen to what I say — you will fall in. This enchanting airy dizziness — you will fall —
the moon a marble well,
shadows move and silent wings, mysterious voices — do you not hear them?

Fathomless the fall
fathomless the climb
the ethereal statue taut with open wings,
fathomless the implacable charity of silence —

lights flickering on the other shore as you swing to and fro in the same wave,
breath of the ocean. Enchanting, airy
this dizziness — take care, you will fall. Don't look at me,
my part is to vacillate — exquisite dizziness. Every night
I have this slight headache, a touch of giddiness.

Often I run across to the chemist for an aspirin,
at other times I cannot stir myself and I am left with my headache
to hear inside the walls the hollow sound of the water-pipes
or I brew a coffee, and always absent-minded,
I forget and prepare two — who is to drink the other? —
silly really, I leave it on the window-sill to get cold
or sometimes I also drink the second, gazing out the window at the chemist's
      green globe
like the green light of a silent train coming to take me
with my handkerchiefs, my worn misshapen shoes, my black handbag, and my poems,
but not suitcases — why would you need them?
Let me come with you.

Ah, you are leaving? Goodnight. No, I won't come. Goodnight.
I'll go out in a little while. Thank you. Because I must
get out of this crumbling house at last.
I should see something of the town — no, not the moon —
the town with its callused hands, the town of the daily wage,
the town that swears by bread and its fist,
the town that bears us all on her back
with our pettiness, our vices, our hates,
with our ambitions, our ignorance, and our old age —
to hear the town's loud footsteps,
not your footsteps anymore
nor God's footsteps, nor my own footsteps. Goodnight.

> The room darkens. A cloud seems to have hidden the moon. Immediately, as if a hand had turned up the radio in the neighbouring bar, a very well-known musical phrase is heard. And then I realise that this whole scene has been softly accompanied by the *Moonlight Sonata*, the first part only. The young man will now descend with an ironic and perhaps compassionate smile on his well defined lips, and with a feeling of liberation. Just as he arrives at Saint Nicholas, before going down the

marble steps, he will laugh — a loud laugh, unrestrained. His laugh will not sound at all unseemly beneath the moon. (Perhaps the only unseemliness is that it isn't unseemly.) The young man will shortly fall silent, become serious and say: "The decline of an era." So, very calmly now, he will unbutton his shirt again and go on his way. As for the woman in black, I don't know if she went out of the house. The moon is shining again. And in the corners of the room shadows huddle together in unbearable regret, in anger almost, not so much against life, as against the useless confession. Can you hear? The radio continues:

Athens, June 1956

YANNIS RITSOS

Farewell

The last hours of Grigoris Afxendiou in the burning cave

DEDICATED
to
the Hero and Saint
GRIGORIS AFXENDIOU
to
the Glorious Dead Poets
and
Teachers of the Nation
DIONYSIOS SOLOMOS
ANDREAS KALVOS
KOSTIS PALAMAS
ANGELOS SIKELIANOS
and to
all the Known and Unknown Martyrs
of Greek and World Struggles

— ◆ —

(Grigoris Afxendiou trapped in the cave at Machairas monastery)

The lies are over at last — ours and theirs.
The cleansing fire comes nearer. Now you cannot
see if it's lentisk, fern, or thyme that's burning. The fire comes nearer.

Yet I must have time to see,
to discern, to reckon, to think — (about whom? about myself? about others?) — I must.
Before my death, now at the last moment, I need
to understand my death, so that I can die.

The other four have gone. Fare you well. How silent it is —
as if a child were about to be born or a martyr to die; and you wait

to hear an enormous cry (from the child or from God) a cry greater than silence
that will hurl down the walls of before, after, and now; so you can
remember, foretell, live everything in one timeless moment. But nothing happens.
Petrified silence — despite the rifle shots and
the voices — how strange they are; you can't hear them; they are carved out
dry as barbed wire or waters that crystallize before they fall
and remain in a strange place, suspended and sharp. How silent it is —
although you can hear the fire approaching. There's no time now to go back —

Behind, beside, and above me, the stone barrier; before me
a quick death or a slow one; in the middle
(in the middle?) myself. — Who am I? — What kind of
man is this, trapped by fire and stone, whose only exit:
an endless death or death at once? I must know him. I haven't time.

— ◆ —

Perhaps I could escape. Perhaps I could
endure the scorn or the forgiveness or even the forgetfulness of others. But would I be able
to forget the light we dreamed of together? That great heartbeat of our flag? Could I
settle down in a shadowy corner with hands crossed on my crossed knees
like a resentful, complaining or aloof spider
that weaves its web with its saliva only?

Perhaps, even then, it would be beautiful —
a stray butterfly might come sometimes and sit on the window bars
fluttering, not for me (but maybe for me too), her delicate little twin flags;
a thin beam of light perhaps would come through the chink in the door like a girl's small finger
reproachfully drawing a line on your dusty table covered with notebooks.
The familiar voice of a child would be heard in the fields one afternoon
and the glance of a woman, smilingly dreaming — her glance, lost in the evening, would touch you,
the glance of a woman who did not see you and whom you saw.

Perhaps it would still be good. A lamp bulb lighting early in front of the barred door of your prison
in the rosy spring evening could be
the gentle curve of the whole shore; the insects would gather on top of it
like little boats in a small harbour of our island.

FAREWELL

You can travel everywhere and be motionless.
Only at the last halt is there no travelling. I couldn't leave.
There wasn't room. The exit was narrow. And my courage failed me
lest I wouldn't be able to die. Forgive me.
Perhaps my four companions were stronger than me — or more honest.
But I was weak: I am ashamed.

— ◆ —

You are going. (They have left.) I'm not keeping you. (They have gone already.) Fare
    you well.
The fire comes nearer. Forgive me friends for not being able
to follow you, for leaving you alone at this exit.
It's the first time. I couldn't. Forgive me.

Yet still I feel I could live anywhere,
in the desert like a bare stubborn rock, forgotten,
or be wronged, do wrong, see my friends wronged and be silent,
or like a beaten mangy dog gaze distrustfully at the shadow of a sparrow and its own
    shadow,
or (I have read about this) lead an ascetic life polishing with the tips of my fingers
(softened at last by disuse) polishing a stone
and oblivious for hours gaze at its immobile veins and bent over like this
silently weep for happiness that I exist. I couldn't.

Suppose I went out giving up my keys, crawling
on my hands and knees (every exit is narrow my friends) suppose I went
to give up my soul like a torn flag — what soul?
I haven't time to try it all out, to know it entirely. I need
this moment to understand what I am giving up or not giving up, and why. I know
that I could have been in your place, my brothers who left,
because I know, as you do, what pain and fear mean,
but I had a fear greater than my pain and your fear,
not just fear for my body, but fear for my soul which I do not know —
the shadow of my every movement grew vast on a fearfully white wall,
and I heard each pulse beat fall into the evermore
inscribing strong watery endless circles. So
with this fear for my soul I escaped from fear for my body. I know however
all of fear and you can believe me
because there is not one of us who wants anyone to suffer or to fear.

Here at least you can believe me.

Here it is not difficult to love one another. Everything is so difficult
and perhaps because of this it's worth the effort. But I couldn't go on
with the knees of my soul lacerated.
With my body, my feet, and my hands lacerated I could. Forgive me. Farewell.

— ◆ —

They have gone. Silence. Loneliness densely inhabited. Everything dense and dissolved.
    The infinite
without suffering and martyrs. To whom will I speak and why? If only they had at least
    stayed —

I mustn't sink into myself. Let me hold on to myself if only by my voice,
by the echo of my own rifle, that my head can stay up
or even my forehead and eyes. I want to see.

I want to imagine trees, windows, things,
to feel their homely warmth, to face
this great chilling fire approaching. A chair
against the corner of a room can be, I think,
like the inside of a bell tower where the sound of the bell
descends filling the house with Sunday silence. I can't continue.

It resembles the impossible victory without martyrs to proclaim it.

I want to imagine my corpse surrounded by weeping friends and flags at half mast
to be able to resign from my body. No one is with me.
My voice my sole witness — and how can that pass through fire and stone?

I have to manage alone. What a silence! — as if permanent. Explicit. The water flask
reminds me that even now I am not thirsty. I will thirst no more. And yet
my knapsack hangs there on the nail still with a look of
the first evening star above the shore at Lemesos
at the hour when the waiters sprinkle the pavement with rubber hoses
after the fearsome heat of a July day; at the hour
when they bring out the first tables on the quayside for the evening customers;
at the hour when even the slightest noise from the smallest fish nearby in the shallow
    water
calls: "tomorrow, tomorrow, tomorrow".

Yes, I could live anywhere, lonely, forgotten, anywhere,
a veteran, unaccountable, without malice, pleased at the feats of others,

glorious acts that I didn't perform — gazing at
the course of a tardy ant carrying in the purple sunset
a grain of corn bigger than its own size and feeling
the whole earth and the summer inviting me; feeling the warmth from the legs of this
    ant,
and with speechless gratitude for the whole world in my eyes
as I hear eternally that little fish calling: "tomorrow, tomorrow". What tomorrow is
    there today?

— ♦ —

This heat is ice cold. I haven't time. The air is thinning.
And I must use my time. To leave some testament. What's the use?
This fire will burn it. It will NOT burn it.
How difficult it is when life is ending. And I must have time
to live this my last trial, to overcome it, and perhaps to give it
as a gift to others. How? With what? "But I must."

What must I do? Who is speaking? What is he saying? Why? "But I must."
Here duties and needs exist no more. Who is commanding me?
What do they want from me? And who are they? The poor, the wronged, my country,
    the world or myself?
Duties and needs. Yes. Duties and needs.
A red flame inside and out. Blood and air.
They exist. I exist. Let us exist.
We will exist. My moment is a red beacon. I must
connect thoughts with things — so they may exist
tangibly. And I haven't time. Things are fading. I don't see them.
Elusive thoughts alone remain and I must
hold on to these, at least — find some way to give them —

Two crusts of yesterday's bread in my knapsack,
the mess tin dazzled by the fire's breath — my meal cold, untouched —
my wristwatch that stopped at two o'clock this morning — how did I forget to wind it? —
strange that things stop that you know can move,
that even determine your own time, your meetings — there is no other meeting;
when they stop, only then, you hear in their silence, their former movement,
and you almost see their movement there, even after it has vanished
and then you know that their fate is their movement beyond where they stopped.

This snail here climbs unconcerned on the stone
it and its little church together — where is it going? It doesn't care.

Shall I speak to it? Confide in it? It is deaf. As if it has never borrowed from anyone —
> it crawls,
it and its little church together — so I must manage all alone — manage what?
The moment of death is not the most suitable
moment for thinking; and it is the only one
that you have completely, because it is the end,
and here there is no room for contradiction and deceit — what words besides?

— ◆ —

I am just twenty-nine years old and the only thing I know is that I want to live.
I haven't yet had time to think since I haven't had time to live. During the battle
what do you think? I hadn't time. I need at least
this complete moment of mine to live completely. I remember —

It was spring then. We were sitting down at the port in Famagusta,
and I know now — I didn't know then — life was beautiful (and is
perhaps always more beautiful — becomes more beautiful — as we make it so)
the ears of corn, the citrons, the orchards, the houses, the women, the boats were
> beautiful —
it was beautiful when the water's reflections played on the sides of ships — beautiful too
the shadows of ships in the water. The shadows of seagulls passed
above the quayside, above the little round tables at the open air café
with the coffee cups; and as we were chatting, three old friends,
without even raising our heads
we sensed the seagulls above us
and we drank with our coffee some of the fleeting shadow of the seagulls,
a taste of spaciousness, friendship, and freedom.

Ah yes, life is beautiful, and I was beautiful (why was? Am beautiful)
and we can so easily make everything beautiful.
Often in the summer in the burning heat of noon — and in the snow —
I felt life securing her flag with faith in my limbs,
and when fear encircled me still with all its cyclopean shadows
and when the flag of my country that I held in my hands stirred the depths of my heart
as the strong winds rattled it
that other flag was not forgotten. It was beautiful. Now
there is no room for such a thing. I have chosen the fire. My decision has been taken. I
> am ready.

Do you think the gate of death is wider? Here I've come to the end. I don't know about
> beyond.

You can make up the other things and talk about them. I still have one great moment
great as pain in its entirety. I didn't know
that one moment could last so long.
I hadn't imagined that pain could think. All things
have their deep meaning and wait for us to find it. And the world would grow poorer
if a pebble, a cicada or the voice of the milkman at dawn were absent. I have learned
    this.
Perhaps this is what they call heroism;
and yet he they called hero didn't know it?
Does thought perhaps conquer silence, fire, and time
and what is known as fate? I didn't know this. I have learned it. Farewell.

This my most beautiful moment I leave to you my brothers.
This is now my rifle — the brand new weapon of man.
And I love this rifle that burns my hands;
I cool this rifle with . . . — There's no harm in your seeing me weep —
I am very moved by everything and by myself
and even more moved by the discovery of this emotion.

If you knew me at this moment I would deserve your love,
as I love you without dishonour or pride.
But who will pass this moment on to you? Words,
hands, eyes, neither act nor thought can be contained in it —
it is as big as what we call our country
as big as what we call the earth
as big as the whole world; (how changed my voice is) as when
you work by your own will, in the poor man's little field and thirsting at midday
trustingly leave your pickaxe leaning against the trunk of the one and only fig tree
and bending over the stream to drink you see in the murmuring stream
your handsome face, flushed with work, air, youth, and sun,
and you admire your shining eyes in the water, and this doesn't stop you
drinking the water with yourself. You quench your thirst and afterwards raise your head
to the sky as if looking for someone to say thank you to
and heaven and earth are inside and outside you, infinite and dazzling.
And the whole world is yours to give.

This moment will not be repeated, because it is eternity,
and eternity exists; we create it — it does not repeat itself
like something that comes and goes and comes again. So don't weep.
But let me weep because in a short time I can see

that I won't be able to weep any more in the knowledge
of my happiness that I am able to die. Forgive me.

I forgot to tell you the most important thing — that I have just now learned —
death is not so difficult. Indeed the reverse.
And I confirm this now with my blood:
never was Christ so happy
as at the moment when the last nail left him immobile, without killing him,
so that he could gaze at heaven and his sacrifice;
never did Prometheus see the world so calmly and so clearly
as at the moment when the beak of the bird of prey found his eyes,
knowing, only then, that he had become worthy to give light and fire to man,
and again, yes, never was little Grigoris Afxendiou twenty-nine years old so beautiful . . .

— ◆ —

I tell you the number of years I have lived and I weep
knowing that you will add them to the glory of our nation
(may this last weakness of mine be forgiven).
I hear this number on your lips
and I would like to kiss it on your lips.

Perhaps I was young for glory — young perhaps
for such happiness. A right act
is a man's leap up from loneliness. It is the clasp
of a thousand hands and the oath of everyone. I am ready.

No, I do not accept sacrifice for death. I accept it
only for life — for a life
that will no longer demand a sacrifice. I am ready.

— ◆ —

I would never have believed that a narrow cave
could have so much space. It can contain
our country with her olive trees, her shores, her griefs,
her boats, sails wide open in the vigorous air;
it can contain the world with its flags, its dreams, its bells, and its small wild plants. I
　　　breathe
in this stone tunnel whose exit
is the mouth of the sun itself. I know that
through it I will go straight into the world, dead. Do not weep.
And I know now, as never before, that freedom is strong. Farewell.

FAREWELL

At this moment I do not fear words big or small —
I can dry my eyes on our flag
because this I know: in my moment of truth
my fellow fighters will receive from my hands
from out of the mouth of death the burning
flag of unyielding struggle, burning
like a blazing horse able to pass through death and the infinite
like an unquenchable torch throughout the night of slavery, a flag burning
like a great shining chalice for the Eucharist of the world. So I can repeat:

"Take, eat, this is my body and my blood
— the body and blood of Grigoris Afxendiou,
twenty-nine years old, of a poor family, from the village of Lisi, taxi driver by trade
who learned in the Great School of Struggle only as many letters
as make up the word FREEDOM"
and who today, the 2nd of March 1957, was burnt alive in the cave at Moni Makhairas
and exactly today, the 2nd of March on a Saturday — do not forget, comrades —
at two o'clock after midnight in the first three minutes,
little Grigoris was born between the bloodstained knees of the world.

— ◆ —

Ten hours are more than enough for everything
when you have a rifle, some bullets and justice on your side
when you have twenty-nine years of your own and can dispose of them yourself
when you have your own death. Farewell.

I keep saying farewell to you and still I am here. Yes, the greatest act in our lives
is our decision to die, when there is a way out
when you can avoid death and yet choose it
out of respect for and duty towards others beyond your own needs.
Whoever is able to conquer a moment in his life conquers death too. I've learned that.

(My voice sounds quite different today. Is this the voice
you are asking of me? Is this the one I would like you to hear? Is it
alone my true voice? Or your voice? Or the voice of us all?)

Nothing exists before you think and before you act.
Not just to think only or to act only,
but to act and think together. And you, my comrades have helped me so much.
(No one exists alone without the help of another.)

You who will weep for my death helped me to die with my head high.
You who will take my rifle to avenge my death
helped me to die happy for you and for myself.
And those who died before me helped me. As I will help you.

This is not a moment for boasting and heroics,
when you find yourself face to face with death,
and I'm telling you simply, as I would turn the steering wheel of my car on a spring day
to avoid colliding with a cart driven by an inexperienced villager
or not to run into a trusting child playing in the sunshine
or even, yes (and this tenderness does not ill-befit a man about to die)
not to crush a wildflower that went astray and grew in the middle of the road
all innocent and azure like the half closed eye of the world —
yes, I can say it as simply to you as I would turn the steering wheel of my car: man's true
    size
is always measured by the yardstick of freedom. Nothing else. Farewell.

If I regret anything it is that I shall no longer be able to do things for you
(not with fame, or concept, or legend, but with these hands of mine).
Let's say I too could shoot a rifle in the air on the feast of liberation
or load onto a large truck a hundred sacks of bread, two hundred of potatoes,
or carry that old woman's load of sticks in the wood
or lift up the old mule driver's horse that has fallen in the mud one rainy morning
or kick the ball the children of my country are playing with in the field one afternoon
or give my friend a cuff one evening for telling a silly joke
or share out, on a day work went well, a paper bag of sweets among the small children
    in our neighbourhood
or place these strong hands of mine, which today I loved,
on a rustic table in Famagusta
and without looking at my workman's hands, feel
them resting on the stone knee of our friendly world.

— ◆ —

Today I feel a tenderness towards myself knowing that you will love me
today I love and esteem myself
today I smile to myself seeing myself with your brotherly eyes.

I left my weapon for a moment to cool from a drop of water in the stone.
I opened my knapsack and took out my pocket mirror —
yes, I am beautiful — when you love me —

FAREWELL

what I could do for you — when you love me —
what I could do — only now I understand — (and perhaps it is too late;
I have only my death to give you now). For example I could
jolt a tank with a blow of my fist
carve a statue on a mountain in one day — when you love me —
or build a tall school in an hour. I am not joking.
It is not the moment for joking, comrades. I would like to be beautiful inside and out
to be worthy of your love; yes, and let me say this: so that all the lovely girls will
think of me as their man; so that all our young Greek people and children of the world
will think of me as their friend. I have no time left.

If only I had time at least to shave, to trim my moustache a little. But maybe
a beard is starting to grow on my young face. You see
what a child your love makes me? It gives me back my own voice. Think, my brother,
the day after tomorrow in our footprints
young girls will choose their men
children their friends
men their actions
know that you too march with them to the heights,
on a high high mountain on a winding asphalt road
to survey the whole world
towns filled with chimney stacks and observatories and windows,
plains and forests, harbours full of masts,
peaceful aeroplanes, brave eagles and childish kites
with their funny multicoloured tails —
on a high mountain, in a car of the latest model bearing our name perhaps?

And now that I have come to think of it, I wonder if life
doesn't move forward with dark confessions and moments of sincerity
(confession — I've heard tell — and now I remember —
saves, they say, the one who confesses. But the other?
What does it profit you for the other to lift your words on his back like sacks of useless
    stones
without being able to build them at all?) So, life
goes forward with acts and sacrifices — with what they call "natural justice",
not that I know what they call it, yet I've said it.

For myself the only thing I have learned is this: as you hold onto the corner of the table
it is the corner of the table with all its firmness
and when you hold a breast you know that the firmest hands tremble
and then you want to sow thousands of children

to enjoy our world that you yourself have not had time to enjoy
and perhaps, I won't say it, perhaps you know — somewhere deep down you feel —
    that this breast
"is preparing the sweet-tasting milk of courage and freedom".
Surely you must know it. Farewell.

— ◆ —

Come, old mother, don't begin to cry now — No? —
I don't want that. True Greek woman. You say I take your life from you? I leave you
    your pride.
The enemy will not see you bowed. I know. You will say:
"I am proud of my son — better a handful of honourable dust
than my brave boy kneeling". That's it.
    Farewell mother.

    Father
will know me at the mortuary by my sturdy Greek bones, like his own,
and by the cross of my country that I kept as a talisman at my heart. I speak about
    myself
as if I were in love with myself, as if my people were in love with me. Forgive me.
It was you who gave me this right. I thank you.
You, and our love, and my death. I even know
that the one who took the five-thousand pieces of silver
will drink a glass to my memory one evening in a taverna in Paphos
and he will lean over to weep into his glass, because I was a good friend
and perhaps he himself will become a friend of ours one day.

So now, with deep certainty I can say to you
as I drive my car once more straight and neat on an asphalt road in Cyprus
on a calm blue morning — I can say: "Our virtue
is in our usefulness to one another." All right, my brothers. Here
brotherhood for us and for all men is not impossible.
Here differences will vanish in a smile — and it is thus
when you hear, on those summer nights — blue, silver and rose —
in one bright glow of happiness
all the separate home-spun murmurings from the stars both great and small
and you tremble to the depths of your heart and the world trembles
so much that you want to nudge a friend's elbow so that he may listen with you,
or be it the elbow of a stone that it may listen, and you may share your joy.

With this love, I tell you that one day wooden crosses

will bud as roses — yes, and my own burnt, stone cross;
with this love I tell you one day we will convince
those who do wrong and sow hate. This is my mandate —
although at this moment I don't know hate
as if I had never learned it or had forgotten it. Farewell.

— ◆ —

I'm still preparing myself to depart. I'm still here saying farewell to you
as if I had something more to add for the world. As if I had
a little more happiness to offer you from my marrow. I remember —

it was a summer twilight —
I stopped the car in front of a hut. I was thirsty.
An old woman dressed in black gave me a jug of cool water.
"Thanks, grandmother," I said to her. "May you go in freedom, son," she replied.
"May you go in freedom, grandmother," I repeated and felt I owed this freedom to her.
She took off my cap and wiped my forehead with her hand. (You know,
old women can smile too.) And so that's it; each of us owes freedom to all.
Freedom for one alone is worth nothing (if it exists).
It means nothing even to him who possesses it. "Come, farewell, grandmother. May you
    go in freedom so" —
and I rubbed my eyes — the blue dazzle of evening was already falling; I couldn't see
    very well.

And as I set off again with my headlights lowered (as it was still daylight)
I felt as if I were climbing up in my car and with me the great plain of Mesaorias
deep and silent, dissolving in the lingering moonlight,
I felt I was climbing up to the sky
and I felt the cool moon strike my chest
as if it were a gold sovereign hanging on a string around my neck,
to refresh my heart and slowly warm itself to dissolve in my body. And I was thinking:
food is not enough, nor money in your pocket, nor bread nor the kiss —
man is greater than his everyday cares. And I was thinking too
that man begins by worrying about bread
and is moving all the time beyond his slavery
from slavery to slavery, from disenslavement to disenslavement,
from disenslavement of his country to disenslavement of the world
until going straight into heaven he feels
the moon evaporating in his body,
until he cries one night for love of the whole world. So I left my car
in a ditch. I took up my rifle. And I went up to the mountain and so I was found

in this cave whose mouth looks straight at the sun. Its round mouth
is the sun itself that will cool me again as they carry me out,
(like the moon on that night) — I will feel it cool as a sovereign
cooling my burnt breast and thus the sun
slowly warming itself will dissolve in our breast. Farewell.

— ◆ —

(All the bells on the earth rang together. All heads were high. All hearts mourned. In the village of Lisi between Nicosia and Famagusta his mother tightened her black kerchief under her firm chin and said exactly the words her son expected of her. "I am proud. Better a handful of honourable dust than my brave boy kneeling." And again his father, when he went to the military hospital in Nicosia, recognised his burnt child by his strong Greek bones and by that gold sovereign dissolving in his breast and in the breast of the world.)

Athens, 5–25 March 1957.

YANNIS RITSOS

The prison tree and the women

To Zizi Makri for her woodcuts

It is evening. The lights-out has sounded a long time ago. The women — gathered in the room, in the dark — are not yet asleep. The sheets on the plank beds shine faintly. Before the women lie down, they sit in a semicircle on the floor, as if around an invisible well, and talk to one another very softly, almost inaudibly. Although they remain motionless, they seem to move in the rhythmic dance of an ancient tragedy. Helen does not speak. She lets down her long black hair and stands in front of the iron-barred window.

ALL THE WOMEN TOGETHER:
   A yard, a tree, a little sun in the morning on the wall — this tree is our calendar, our friend, our postman, our child,
FIRST WOMAN:
   sometimes even our husband — not sometimes —
SECOND WOMAN:
   often, very often — our husband; through it we take part in the year,
THIRD WOMAN:
   we take part in the cycle of time and in memory
FOURTH WOMAN:
   and even in what is called change and renewal. This tree at the centre of our yard, at the centre of our emptiness, insists on being; insists on noticing, perceiving, responding;
FIFTH WOMAN:
   bound beneath, to climb upwards,
FOURTH WOMAN:
   divided into four seasons to unite seasons and landscapes;
FIRST WOMAN:
   sometimes it looks on our behalf outside the wall,
THIRD WOMAN:
   it absorbs the voice of the child selling matches,

SECOND WOMAN:
: the voice of the ice-man,

FOURTH WOMAN:
: the silence of the woman who has bought five roses from the corner flowershop,

FIFTH WOMAN:
: the footstep of a man reading a newspaper on the pavement,

ALL TOGETHER:
: not counting the colours of so many different hours, indeed many colours during the course of the day,

FIRST WOMAN:
: and the stars during the course of the night — strange stars, notched wheels, pentagrams, carriages, calm animals, and the two bullock-carts of clouds stopped at the castle-gate of the moon.

THIRD WOMAN:
: No-one was living on the moon;

SECOND WOMAN:
: perhaps he was sleeping, perhaps pretending to sleep;

FIRST WOMAN:
: the keys heard in the big corridor,

FIFTH WOMAN:
: a white stab in the dark,

FOURTH WOMAN:
: and it was so simple, almost trivial, unimportant being or not being. Such simplicity this tree taught us — this is our wisdom,

ALL TOGETHER:
: this is our quiet courage: to be absent, to expect, not to expect — the silent joy in offering ourselves when others forget or don't even know —

FIRST WOMAN:
: simple, humble, noble understanding,

SECOND WOMAN:
: like the stone in the hand-hewn wall,

THIRD WOMAN:
: like the log in the fire,

FIFTH WOMAN:
: like the pane in the window; the modest window-pane, without pride, unseen, it helps others to see,

THIRD WOMAN:
: it makes things clear, protects from the wind,

SECOND WOMAN:
   protects from the cold, it lets the light through and the heat —
FOURTH WOMAN:
   a thin, transparent solitude, which protects from solitude, a short silence between two bitter words — you have time to think — the second bitter word is not said;
ALL TOGETHER:
   the wind clears, the eye clears, all is clear — silent understanding, distant, close understanding —
FOURTH WOMAN:
   this is our most humble greatness, and it is not difficult for us to say this word, but that we are silent we, held here, locked up, pensioned off from events,
FIRST WOMAN:
   shut in from without. But the tree observes and sees outside on our behalf, and then
ALL TOGETHER:
   the tree passes into us —
FIFTH WOMAN:
   many times, during sleep, lying down, we remain standing in the posture of the tree — perhaps this tree must not let us rest,
FIRST WOMAN:
   must not let us forget,
FOURTH WOMAN:
   must not let us die.
FIFTH WOMAN:
   This tree keeps watch without effort or display.
FIRST WOMAN:
   Its most delicate branches spread in our fingers;
FIFTH WOMAN:
   when we eat, a yellow leaf happens to fall next to the bread from Mary's hands — none of us is surprised — and sometimes a small green twig happens to move under the black kerchief of Aunt Costenna.
SECOND WOMAN:
   Or a white flower falls from Ismini's eyes into our meal in the saucepan — and we are not surprised,
ALL TOGETHER:
   we put this flower aside with our knife and silent, continue our supper,

FOURTH WOMAN:
> knowing however with certainty that spring is approaching, that there are many stars, many trees

FIFTH WOMAN:
> many people, much grief, much courage behind the walls,

THIRD WOMAN:
> many walls behind the walls,

FIRST WOMAN:
> and much sky above the walls,

THIRD WOMAN:
> and hope? And hope?

ALL TOGETHER:
> Don't speak — be quiet, quiet.

THIRD WOMAN:
> A knock on the wall by an unseen hand is fear, a spider beneath the piled up leaves, a knock — they are nailing the door — they are nailing us in,

FIRST WOMAN:
> yes, a knock — they are driving a nail in the door to hang . . .

THIRD WOMAN:
> A nail in the door is death — there, it waits — the nail rusts in the damp — it waits

FIRST WOMAN:
> for them to hang up wreaths of flowers for May Day. May is approaching;

THIRD WOMAN:
> the flowers hid the nail, but it is beneath the flowers —

SECOND WOMAN:
> and how else would they hang the wreaths? Quiet.

THIRD WOMAN:
> And beneath the rusted nail — the darkened blood —

ALL TOGETHER:
> this is not our May; our May takes long strides, has drums and smoke and flags,

THIRD WOMAN:
> and the darkened blood in the shadow cast by the flags —

FOURTH WOMAN:
> living veins spread out on the flags — a great body above the shadow of death — its shape a prow,

FIFTH WOMAN:
> it rends the air — a high, high mast,

FIRST WOMAN:
: and the rope ladder tied to the sun —

SECOND WOMAN:
: a tang of the sea and pelargonium — do you not feel it? The smarting in the nostrils — two small semicircles of salt?

ALL TOGETHER:
: It is the smell of the world — the great immeasurable circle —

FOURTH WOMAN:
: the smarting, yes, just inside the nose, as when you sneeze looking straight at the sun — do you not feel it?

FIRST WOMAN:
: There are the flags — they rattle in the air like great doors opening —

THIRD WOMAN:
: and we, here, behind the walls, without flags,

ALL TOGETHER:
: and we to our tasks behind the walls, transforming the motionless tree into a thousand moving leaves, transforming the separate movements into indivisible simplicity, into an eternity almost.

FIRST WOMAN:
: Look, Helen is sitting at the window, she is looking beyond, she is looking at the blue mist rising from the stones in the garden, she taps her finger on the bars of the window — a deep sound, quiet — a little rhythm of our own —

ALL TOGETHER:
: this is the knock you hear — listen, listen;

FIRST WOMAN:
: the sound comes out of the bars, out of the stones,

SECOND WOMAN:
: the pulse of spring in the iron vein, in the stone vein

FOURTH WOMAN:
: a little wireless, hidden, gives the signal —

THIRD WOMAN:
: and we entangled in the branches of the dark with elbows fixed to the sides of silence, to the damp of the night, waiting the reply — what reply — waiting —

ALL TOGETHER:
: And the reply comes

SECOND WOMAN:
: sometimes from the last bird at dusk,

FIFTH WOMAN:
: sometimes from a cricket sawing the night,

FIRST WOMAN:
>sometimes from a star that repeats: "I come, I come, I come",

THIRD WOMAN:
>sometimes from a torn love letter that a sudden wind tosses in the street —

FOURTH WOMAN:
>we listen within and without — another time exists with time, with trees and windows multiplied,

THIRD WOMAN:
>and with walls multiplied,

FOURTH WOMAN:
>yes, and with walls — why not? — with many windows,

FIRST WOMAN:
>suddenly the door handle gleams like a great drop of water,

SECOND WOMAN:
>and a curved landscape gleams in the water-drop

THIRD WOMAN:
>and the naked jaw of a horse gleams above it.

ALL TOGETHER:
>Be quiet, quiet. Look, Helen's back, turned to us, is a knoll with little cypress trees,

FIFTH WOMAN:
>there a flock of white sheep ascends — the night turns grey,

FIRST WOMAN:
>because the stars are coming out,

SECOND WOMAN:
>because we are waiting,

THIRD WOMAN:
>because the spring is coming again — why is it coming? As day dawns we stand in a row, one by one, in front of the illumined square of wall,

FOURTH WOMAN:
>patiently, silently, in order,

THIRD WOMAN:
>one by one in her turn — each one alone,

FOURTH WOMAN:
>one by one, and all together, to gather a little sunshine,

ALL TOGETHER:
>one by one, in order, while all our shadows flow into one another, criss-cross on the ground in dark and luminous rhombuses, till they merge in a single well. Opposite the well this tree stands upright once more on our behalf.

FIRST WOMAN:
    And we, we stay silent and listen leaf by leaf, to beyond and further beyond,
SECOND WOMAN:
    and green leaves peep out of Mary's hair — so much that we are afraid they will be seen, the keys will sound in the guard's belt, a glass will fall from above and break on the paving stones,
ALL TOGETHER:
    the words we concealed will be heard — perhaps for this reason sparrows are so clumsy sometimes when they hop along the ground.

The women lay down. Outside the walls and in the room there were many stars, indescribably many stars, like notched wheels, like pentagrams, like carriages, like calm animals, like birds, like broad leaves — and they shone so much that Helen was unable to sleep. So she covered her face with her long black hair, while opposite, that single tree glowed with all its leaves, in the middle of the world and its shadow climbed on the wall of the prison like a huge ladder. Everyone could climb it. And, yes, it was spring.

Prague, September 1962

YANNIS RITSOS

from
Twelve poems on Cavafy

THE POET'S ROOM

The black, carved desk, the two silver candlesticks,
his red pipe. He sits, invisible almost,
in the armchair, his back always to the window. Behind
huge glasses he warily observes each visitor
on whom the full light falls, himself hidden among his words,
behind his masks in history, far off, invulnerable,
ensnaring attention in the subtle glow
of a sapphire ring on his finger: he is ready
to savour their phrases, as callow adolescents
moisten their lips admiringly with their tongue. And he sits there,
voracious, crafty, carnal, the one without sin,
wavering, his whole being like scales in the hand of the god
wavering between yes and no, desire and remorse,
while the light from the window behind his head
invests him with a crown of pardon and saintliness.
"If poetry is not absolution" — he whispers to himself —
"then let's not look for mercy anywhere."

YANNIS RITSOS

from
The fourth dimension

AJAX

A tall, strongly built man is lying on the floor surrounded by broken crockery, saucepans, and slaughtered animals — cats, dogs, hens, lambs, goats, a donkey, two horses, and a white ram tied upright to a post, like a captive tied to the stake. He is wearing a white nightgown, rather like an ancient tunic; blood-stained and torn, it leaves his sturdy body almost uncovered. He looks tired as if just recovering from an all-night drinking bout. On his face there is an expression of helplessness and grief, ill-matched with, and even at odds with, his physical proportions and the taut muscles of his forearms, thighs, and calves. A woman, with foreign features, pale, watchful, frightened, and perhaps secretly angry, stands silent in front of the door. Her posture is rather strange — as if she were hiding a young child behind her. Dawn has broken some time ago. Outside, the light is strong. Here inside through the closed shutters, a sickly reflection crawls over the walls. The cries of fruit-sellers, knife-grinders, and fishmongers can be heard, and down below on the shore the shouts of sailors sluicing the decks and tidying their boats at the moorings. The man is motionless on the floor. One cannot tell where he is looking or what he sees. He speaks slowly, wearily and sometimes feverishly or fearfully.

"Woman, what are you staring at? Close the doors, close the windows, draw the bolt,
fill the cracks, venomous insects are coming in, lizards,
big flies are coming in, and secret laughter. Look, on the wall,
a black fly, black, black, getting bigger, blackening the day,
breathing black air — cover it with your hand, kill it,
I can't look at it. Why don't you speak? Well then, look at me —

The strong one, the unconquerable one — you loaded me with eulogies,
you burdened me, you suffocated me — one by one and all together hanging
round my neck — you suffocated me. Look at your work. Rejoice if you want. Nobody
allowed me to be tired for one hour; nobody
allowed me to be ill. And you, your slightest little

worries magnified, you throw them on my back —
all the time complaining and bewailing; the maid is infatuated with a sailor,
the other one's wearing a silk jacket, she's putting black on her eyes to make them
        look bigger,
she's painting her nails cyclamen, the third one, the youngest,
has put her hair up, she's lost the soap in the wash-tub,
the lettuce has shrivelled, the coal's going down, your worries,
you go over and over them at supper, at that quiet hour
when battles and quarrels cease, and each of us seeks
a cool drop of forgetfulness, yielding to our body's needs
among the plates, the glasses shining gently and peacefully beneath the oil lamps —
and you, all the time grimacing, panting, waving your arms,
opening a huge mouth, gulping the air, the stars —
and a cunning little star like a silver chick-pea; I think,
now it'll stop at her larynx, she'll sneeze, she'll choke, and be silent.

Even at the hour for love, at night, in bed, suddenly you would
remember that the clothes pegs were left in the yard
and they'll rot in the damp. Agh foolish women — that's how
you drive us away from the bed, from the house, from the world,
away from your wise and practical minds, honed by
recipes for desserts, drinks, potions; you drive us away
from life itself with the little, sacred, everyday happenings,
the little, tangible objects resting from the big elusive things.

Not one of you ever asked me what I was thinking or feeling, what terrors,
what injustices, what malice I faced (the fearless one, you see) or even
if I had a sore tooth or a headache, as if I hadn't
teeth or a head, as if I were stone or mere air. Why are you staring at me like that?
Close the doors, close the windows, draw the bolt.
There's the black fly, look, on the ox's horn sharpening its nails.

Oh yes, the strong one, the unconquerable one; look at me. Nobody
ever asked for a share of my troubles. You — the innocent,
the astute, the despairing, and the crafty, for me
you had nothing but self-seeking admiration, not love,
only clamouring admiration. And you even became angry
any time I fell ill, as if I had betrayed you. And indeed I did betray you,
since I had betrayed myself. Here I am huddled on the ground; and my enemies
mocking me, sniggering at me. All last night,
they were spying on me all round the house; they could see me. They were looking

through the shutters, through the curtains, through the key-holes, out of the cupboards.
I heard the creaking on the floor, the scratching on the wall. When I went out
they hid behind the trees. They were watching me. A white moon

huge, white as calico cloth, was rising from Mount Ida; a white frost
covered my eyes; then I was remembering something — what was it? — a white
        handkerchief
like in "blind man's buff" that we used to play as children in Salamina; you couldn't tell
who was calling or from where they were calling you in a strange voice — as if you were
in a big, dark church on a burning hot day and the tall
pale icons were saying something in low voices to one another about you —
a huge snake, a lion with a thorn in its paw,
a severed head on a plate, two frightened eyes,
a big eye all alone, beards, blood dripping
from the tip of the spear, smoke, burnt laurel, little bells. I thought I'd go back —

Which way forward? Which way back? The moon had whitewashed the road;
the whole road was shining and I looked enormous; they could see me
from everywhere. How could I go back? Even my shadow
had abandoned me — it had melted in the glare of the whitewash —
as if it were salt. Big octopuses, dried out, stretched out
on canes hung on the walls. One moment my sword
would get bigger, gleaming brighter and brighter,
too heavy for me to lift, lighting me up from head to foot
and then it would get very small, like the pared fingernail of a child.
Close the doors, close the windows, draw the bolt.

All the houses locked — they had shut me out. Copper rings
shone on the doors. Big barrel hoops were rolling down
from the hills — coming to trap me. The huge moon was rolling in circles
gouging a dry well for me to fall in. I could neither
walk nor stand. I could hear my footsteps on the cobbles
strange, resolute, betraying, until at the port below
I heard the chain my feet were dragging and everything went silent.

Then all paths out were closed to me — ropes worn away, noises disguised;
up in the camps they had put out the fires; all around, the enclosures
sparked with little clay pipes. Big masks
hung in the air — it was them, in the neighbours' yards
it was them wearing cardboard carnival masks — oxen, donkeys,
horses, sheep — they couldn't escape from me now;

they walked on all fours pretending to be quadrupeds — they didn't make a sound;
they crawled on the ground like huge infants. The silence curved
over me like a glass bell — I was afraid I'd break it. Then suddenly,
from a thousand secret corners I heard them calling my name — horribly,
again and again my name booming in the water-pipes, in the empty jars,
in the toilet bowls, in the chimneys; my name —
some of them called from far way in women's voices and others close to me in a
           thundering voice
imitating my own voice "Ajax, Ajax, Ajax"
in fatuous boastfulness "Ajax, Ajax", so that
I hate my name for ever — Oh, not to hear it again,
no-one to utter it again; oh to be anonymous, forgotten,
strapped to the belly of my horse. Then I couldn't bear it.
I raised my sword and struck, I rounded them up
and dragged them in here — look at them — they were these animals.
Close the doors, close the windows, draw the bolt.

Woman, why are you staring like that? The fly — kill it.
Am I not a human being too? Why then? All night
you also were spying on me behind the door, yes, with my son —
you were showing me to the child, so he could see me helpless here — no, no,
you covered his eyes with your hands so that he wouldn't see. All night
bronze arrows stuck in the walls, trembled, endlessly
echoing every sound — my footstep, my breathing, my pulse,
the clothes rubbing against my knee, my breast — how could I escape?
What to protect myself against first? My enemies had pierced me with arrows,
secret antennae following my movements. I seized them. One
I grabbed by the ear; I dragged him in. His ear grew longer
and longer as I dragged him, while he stayed out there.

Another one sank his teeth in my thigh — the mad dog; those cunning Atreides —
and Tevkros gone to the mountains. I called; "Tevkro, Tevkro";
I had no voice. I called again. The earth vanished under my feet. I had
nothing to hold on to, not even my own belt* —
as I was blindly searching for it, I suddenly realised it was severed,
and instead of holding me, I was holding it in my hand
like the flayed tail of a strange, incredible animal.
Close the doors, close the windows, draw the bolt.

*The belt Ajax had given to Hector when they stopped the duel in which they were both equally matched. Achilles used this belt to tie the feet of the dead Hector to his chariot.

THE FOURTH DIMENSION : AJAX

This night has passed. I feel better now. Don't be frightened woman.
I went out again at dawn. I saw you standing watching at the door.
I went down to the shore before the sailors awoke.
I cupped some water in my hands and bathed my temples. How small dear God,
how small we are against the vast, awakening world,
against the blue, eternal light. And suddenly I felt
the curse and terror of the night fading — and as I crouched,
small, among the rocks in beautiful, silent grief,
and pity for myself — gazing at the motionless ships,
seeing again, and knowing that I see — and hearing again — I was happy.

One boat was girdled in red; its reflection
in the water even redder, like the glow of a dying fire,
and I thought again: "like the glow of a dying fire" — an exquisite thrill
unclenched my teeth and my knees because of that little word "like" — because I could
put one thing beside another again. I could speak, I could transform things —
"like the glow of a dying fire", and it didn't burn me. How peaceful
the solitary creaking of planks and ropes in the breathing water — the peaceful
creaking of invisible oars and oarlocks, rowing me
secretly far away, forgotten, without a single weapon.

Then a flock of seagulls rose near me — a white trembling
shield sheltered me, gentle, ethereal, courteous wings
moving confidently in the air — big, friendly palms
soundlessly applauding the silence, brushing against my shoulder
with trust again — yes, a new trust. So don't grieve.

I assure you I'm calm now — I seek neither the death
of others nor my own death. I no longer care about
the deceit of the gods or my self-deception or the derision
of my comrades — I'm far away, it can't reach me. What can I do
with pointless booty and the big shield and spear?
Protect myself against what? And in what way? The Trojans didn't break me —
fear of the enemy is nothing against fear of the friend
who knows your secret wounds and aims for them. I lay on the shore
watching the pale, shadowy dawn, without the burden
of expectation or hope. Man's heart
is a moist root in the earth, patient, hidden
so deep — then spring comes — and it can put out shoots again.

I saw the tents shining in the humid dawn; a grey

and rose-coloured light, like a convalescent, trailed over the stones. I remembered
other mornings, long gone, unsuspecting mornings, full of urgent hurry and the noise
of anchors, oars, cauldrons, pulleys, when the sailors
risen early would urinate on the shore, all in a row,
and that rose-coloured light, on the horizon, on the shores,
on their hands, their faces, their penises, trembled as if enchanted
so that we, not meaning to, would look down at the water and see ourselves
          reflected there
and fall in love again with our bodies in all their fearless bravery
until out of the sea rose the huge spectre of the sun
and we lost ourselves again in battles and empty vainglory.

I don't want any of that — what's to be gained from it? — I can do without it.
My old feats seem like lies to me now. All the rewards
that were due to me, others appropriated through fraudulent
drawing of lots and briberies; then I, at the time when the life of the Greeks hung in
          the balance,
threw into the helmet not damp lumps of earth
but my big, easily visible wedding-ring and went out first
against the enemy man to man. And again, when the ships
were burning and the smoke and flames were rising to the skies
and you'd think the sea was burning, when Hector
in deadly rage was swooping on the trenches it was I again
who was in front. It seems the Atreides don't remember this.
They cared only for booty and rewards. Well let them profit
by cunning, deception, and fear — for how long? One day
they too will stand naked before the night and its long road;
the stolen shield, so big and fine will be useless to them then.

Above the shore, all over the hills, the clothes
of the dead warriors rotted; shoes warped, buckles rusted
in the damp and the rain; little by little they have become
a thick, soft layer; up there in spring thousands of wild multicoloured
flowers appear — perhaps they take their colours
from the clothes of the dead. If you walk on them you feel
a deep, peaceful softness — not the softness of decay and depletion, no,
another softness, as of something ended or non-existent. You bite a leaf;
it has no taste. You pluck a flower; you look at it;
you can see among its petals a transparent landscape in the colour and shape
of the flower — everything is hollow, in a deep hollowness. In one step
you can cross to the other side with the quiet poplars and the white river.

THE FOURTH DIMENSION : AJAX

Those who have gone return to us silently, by the shortest roads,
over the hills with the olive-trees, through the vineyards —
I saw them when I was returning home. They nodded to me. The chimneys
were like black statues on the roofs. They were passing by
dark, dark and mute, like trees on a river bank traced
on a bright stretch of water. A white moon
stands above them all day long — it doesn't shine on them. They cross the road;
in newsagents' shops they look at sweets wrapped in muslin;
they look at cardboard dolls on strings, at cigarettes, matches,
hair-clips, newspapers — they don't even read the names. They look at themselves
in the dusty window of the bakery. Like dry grass
their hair falls on their cheeks, their chins, their shoulders.

Their hands are long and wasted — they can't hold
shields and bows — nor do they think of it — nor do they attempt to change
the relaxed expression on their lips. Unrestricted, invisible,
with that pleasing austerity throughout their bearing, in harmony
with their beautiful movements, with the absence of all anxiety,
in their slow, unending time. Immune. I envied them.

On the bridge they met a band of gipsies. Nobody
saw them. It was just that the rustle of yellow skirts stopped
at once, and the coffee-mills suddenly glittered
with gold-red sparks. The seven pitch-back horses
bent their heads to the ground; they pricked up their ears. It was just that
the huge bear with the rings stood on her hind legs
in the middle of the bridge, blocking everyone's way.

She wasn't going to move from there — she was looking behind her, sniffing
    the air —
a smell of brimstone and incense and grape. Her eyes
big, dark, unfathomable. Many times they had to pull
her strap; they lifted the whips to her. She set off,
now and then turning her head, looking back, as I did too.

The shadow of a bird passed at my feet — I didn't raise my eyes —
a distant sympathy and forgiveness. And I wished for
a little peace — not glory, not glory. Take away these slaughtered lambs and oxen —
lambs and oxen, yes, and my enemies remain intact to mock at me.
Take them away from here — I can't look at them. Agh, it was always the same;

I spent all my strength fighting phantoms, winning entirely
imaginary victories, conquering non-existent gold cities,
non-existent, non-existent. So, lambs and oxen. Nothing more.

All last night you also heard their pitiful cries.
Look at that white ram — how peaceful, how sad
its eyes, dear God — a little Saint John — those eyes
taught me gentle humility. Let the Atreides laugh as much as they like
at my "impetuous feats of valour" and at the other, real ones
that I once performed for Greece and for the Greeks — one day they will
    remember me.

Or not, as they wish. Does it matter? In losing everything
what I have found is enough for me. Soon I shall go
and wash myself in the river, wash my sword. It would be good
to embalm these animals — especially this white ram —
but how to preserve its expression? In its eyes
the door shines much smaller, and the morning, two leaves,
and a tiny dot of light — perhaps that's the fountain
where Achilles watered his horses. Throw them out of here. Why are you still
    keeping them?
Close the doors, close the windows, draw the bolt.

Listen — they're laughing again in the yard. Aren't they? Quiet. Quiet.
Woman, I'm cold. Bring me a blanket. Cover me.
Isn't it cold don't you think? Are your teeth chattering too?
How good it would be to become smaller and smaller and smaller,
all coiled up, immovable, covered, hidden
under your fallen shield, it too rusted by the rains and the salt air,
with its old heroic scenes all faded away, and lying under it
to pull its strap to the ground and so become one with the earth —

Agh, and straining all the time to hear if someone's passing
for fear they'll kick the shield by accident, and the sound of the metal close to your ear,
clang-clang, the great clash of arms; your blood will drain away; only the terrible
clash of arms coursing in your veins ringing endlessly deep inside you
clang, clang — making your contortions audible to everyone, revealing
the shape of your humiliation — I hear this sound, it conquers me
like the betrayal of myself by myself,
that self whom I had trained and strengthened
with illusion and the pride of invincible courage — what courage,

when deeper within us, our alien life and alien death lay claim to us?
No, it's not humiliation. If I was defeated, I was defeated
not by men, only by the gods. No victory is our own and no defeat.
Close the doors, close the windows, draw the bolt.

Agh, nothing is ours — whatever we achieve and whatever we are, someone else
gave to us and takes it back again; some stranger, unknown to us, without our consent.
That fly buzzing and buzzing — kill it. A strange foot
has hit again against the fallen shield — Do you hear? Clang, clang — the shield —
clang, clang — it's going away, it's gone. It was nothing. Take the blanket. I'm not cold.
Just this humming in my temples here and the shadow rippling on the wall —
going round and around notch by notch — around and around again.

I want to remember something good — a radiant day in Salamina
when they were caulking the new ships at the shore, and a fragrance
of planed wood wafted on the air, and further up in the little pine grove
the cicadas in a frenzy. I want to remember. I can't. My memory breaks off in the middle;
everything sinks into that chasm; only the bad things stay on the outside —
the enemy's flashlight in your eyes when you're sleeping,
the iron on the feet, the harpoon in the temples, the cries of the wounded
at night in the gorge, with the jackals, and my own cry
come from far away to my own ear. I can't. I look all around. I can't see.

I want to see above the backs of these slaughtered animals. "A tree," I say:
"a tree," I reply. That's it. Nothing more. The tree disappears. It wasn't there.
Even my body — repulsive, I don't want to touch it —
a loathsome thing — alien, strange; a smell of goat — what is the human body?
Just pores — nothing else — looking into a slimy darkness;
the hair rough like dried out rushes; behind the rushes
a big unrecognisable rotting carcass — with a strong jaw,
a naked jaw, already white, firmly clenched
in a grimace of general discontent and comical menace. And the clenching
of the white jaw with the huge teeth is the only
mark of pride and honour in this lax and boneless body.

What use now are trophies, glory, eulogies. They are nothing.
Failure and mockery are nothing. They vanish with us.
I never asked for slaves, admirers, vassals. I want nothing more than a man
to speak with as an equal — where is he? Only our death
is our equal. Everything else casts an easy lustre on us —
compromise, pretence, turning a blind eye.

Returning here I was stumbling over traces of old fires in the grass —
burnt branches, ashes, charcoal, soot; nearby, lying around, the big skewers
from sacrifices and banquets. Piles of big bones
were whitening in the dawn with a silver-white
of memory or of what is yet to come — infinitely calm
and with something of the undaunted pride
of a distant memorial to those who have died, that is, to us, to ourselves,
and the grass was yellow beyond, yet down below
the sea shimmered absurdly rose-coloured, imposing a motion
all over again — its motion and our motion.

Then I remembered Salamina — pale mornings with mist and drizzle
that effaced everything at last — boats, anchors, taverns, fish shops
and only the road shone silver, all alone, going vaguely onwards somewhere
turning every now and then, and turning about again to avoid invisible obstacles
or for its own pleasure, with that silver-white colour.

In the house I found mother sitting in the dining-room
bending thoughtfully over a fine thread on which she was stringing daisies —
white, blue-tinged, silver. "What will you do with them, mother?" I asked.
And she replied: "I'll throw them into the well." She smiled. "Then
why are you stringing them?" I looked at her. She didn't raise her eyes. "She who
    will wear them
wants them like this," she replied. Then I understood
that in every well, and within us, is a beautiful drowned woman,
a drowned woman who shows no sign of dying — I don't know what it means —
but there she is, patient, so patient, beneath the noise of our horses and carts and
    chariots.

Open the windows, open the door, draw back the bolt.
It's nothing. I'll go out for a little and wash myself in the river. Tell Tevkros —
by the way, where is Tevkros? Tevkro, Tevkro — take these animals away.

I'm going to wash myself, and wash my sword* — and perhaps I'll find a man to
    talk to.
What a beautiful day — ah the light of the sun, the golden river — farewell wife.

*The sword was given to Ajax by Hector during the duel referred to in the note on page 92.

He goes away. The woman stays motionless beside the door. A loud ringing sound is heard, like a hammer hitting a metal disc hanging in another room. Perhaps an invisible foot has hit against the fallen shield with the seven impenetrable layers of ox-hide. The noise continues. The men-servants enter. They gather up the slaughtered animals. And the white ram with the sad eyes. A tall, silent big-boned slave-woman comes in with a large broom. She sweeps up the broken plates, cigarette butts, and trampled coffee pots. Her loose black kerchief covers her face. The room has emptied. It suddenly looks very large. The ringing sound has stopped. Outside, street cries and the activity of the port — cranes, pulleys, chains can now be heard very clearly. Then suddenly a sailor comes running in. "The master," he says. "The master's dying with his sword in his ribs." The woman is motionless at the door; and the tall slave-woman, at the end of the corridor, stands petrified, her hands placed on the shaft of the broom.

LEROS, SAMOS, August 1967 – January 1969

YANNIS RITSOS

Love poems

1

You've come back from the market blithely carrying
bread, fruit, and bunches of flowers. The wind, I see,
has passed its fingers through your hair. I don't love the wind;
I am telling you again. And why do you want so many flowers? Furthermore
which of them all did the flowerseller give you? And perhaps in the mirror
of the flowershop your picture has stayed obliquely lit
by a blue stain on your chin. I don't love flowers. On your breast
a large blossom like a whole day. Sit, then, opposite me;
I want to gaze alone at the fold of your knees and smoke
until secret night falls and above our bed magnetised, a Saturday night
rembetiko moon settles with viola, clarinet and santouri.

2

Erotic sleep after love. Damp sheets
hanging from the bed onto the floor. In my sleep I hear
the loud river. A lingering rhythm. Large tree trunks
roll with it. In their branches thousands of birds
sit motionless travelling in a long song
of water and leaves, interrupted by stars. Gently I
slip my arm beneath your neck, lest I
stop the song of birds in your sleep. Tomorrow, at ten,
when you open the shutters and the sun sweeps into the rooms
there will appear in the mirror more clearly your bitten lower lip
and the house will become bright red, all dotted
with golden down and far-off unconsummated verses.

3

Your body on the beach
the sand clinging to your flesh
the sand on my hands
on my tongue
I want to discover you
behind the most delicate obstacle
and the sand to fall from our hair
sinking to the depths of silence
and we
beautiful freshly bathed
from our own waters rising
into the light and the body
of this earth.

4

Therefore I turn the stone of the ring inwards, I clasp it
in my palm, lest a stranger's envious or innocent glance
cast an evil eye on this inexhaustible happiness within time, outside time
and lest we find next morning in the lift the three slaughtered deer.

5

The sunset gleamed
on the shoulder of a bird.
Together we saw it.
We smiled.
Your hand was in mine.

The house where we lived
follows me.

But
to the right of the road
I saw a wood
mauve and gold.
And the sorrow that you didn't see.

Opposite in the glass door
the snow-covered mountain.

6

You threw off the sheet
you opened the windows,
we were filled with stars.
A golden butterfly in your hair.

You always came
with flowers in your hands.
I waited for you
the flowers and you.
What happened to the gardens?

Night
the stone seat beside the sea.
You took off your sandals.
A ship all lit up
was leaving.

7

A large rose
climbs companionless,
in the dark.

The door-bell rings.
The telephone rings.
Nothing.
We are absent
together.
And the conspiring rain.

The shape of your body
clay
in my hands
becomes a pitcher,
a lecythus,
nine statues,
and an eagle.

8

Put your bare foot
on the paper
on the poem
with the pencil I'll trace
the pattern of your foot
I'll put it on the wall
with a drawing pin
and I'll light the three candles
in the candle stick —
well then, close the door.

from
Responses

THE BLOOD

The lorries passed raising dust.
The sunset shone gold and violet on the window-panes.
The snails gathered round the sacred well. The black bull,
erotic, arrogant, on the hill-top,
breathes in the approaching night. We waited for years.
They didn't come. They didn't send a message. Their empty clothes
are still in the wardrobe. Every night
the wounded pass by on the road with bandages
on their hands, their feet, their foreheads. Drops of blood
sprinkle the pavements. Next day the women with brushes
and buckets of water wash it away. But the blood appears again
redder still in the words we will never say.

HE WITH THE HAT

He was holding his hat on his knee.
The night is mild, silver and rose
with a moon foxy in her right-hand corner.
Ah, he's hiding something under his hat — perhaps
a bird, a snake, or an apple. He doesn't stir.
He avoids looking us in the eye. This
redoubles our suspicions. Suddenly
he gets up, puts on his hat, goes away.
There was nothing under his hat, only
a hole in the sofa and one in the ceiling.
In this hole a star appeared, and then vanished.

FISHING VILLAGE

The poor houses of fishermen, roofs, smoke-stained doors,
a balcony with broken panes, sad caïques,
a little smoke, three anchors, brine and vinegar,
the boats go into the yards, they roost under the trees,
repentant evening, universal, weighed down with ships' sirens
dotted with the shadows of swallows. "Don't leave," he said, "Don't leave.
Let's share the myth of the evening. Afterwards it doesn't matter.
The rowers will overtake the night with a song
and the sound of their oars in our heartbeats."

SUDDEN CHARGE

Empty bottles thrown in the yard
beneath the only quince tree. The underground river
rumbles in the autumn dusk. A denuded tree
impersonates the statue. Words deferred
hover on the lips. At night the three
horsemen entered the Church of Christ-in-Chains
astride their white horses, they stripped
the silver offerings from the Virgin of Tenderness
and then, all dust and trampling, they disappeared beyond
in a rose-coloured cloud dotted with stars.
We, who were still in bed, didn't know what to think —
that beauty — inexplicable, the three white horses
ghostlike, and on them the three slaughtered horsemen.

JUSTIFICATION

The sponge-divers slept under the big clock of the customs house.
The surrounding fields were sown with bones.
The brigands went calmly away, at the hour when a huge moon
was shining on the boat-yard with its half-finished caïques
and a smell of damp wood pervaded the night. The beautiful woman
appeared on the balcony holding in her hands
a bunch of allegorical roses. So we too found
some justification for all our hesitations.

ONE NIGHT

The ambulances passed in the night sounding their horns.
Then the fire-engines. In the woods
they were closing in on the poachers. The antiques smugglers
hidden beneath the bellies of marble horses.
In the next room the woman lying in bed. On the inner door
the compassionate drawings of shadows.
Unrestrained music at the two windows
and the perforated moon. What more
they wanted to say, they didn't say.
And all night, the whole night long, the dark
insidious rumble of the underground river.

CONSOLATORY

Tired people wait smoking,
outside events; they wait in the evening
at the bus-stop, under the shelter,
looking for new pretexts. A young man
stands in front of the stationer's.
In the little square the children are running,
shouting, playing. A little later
night falls immortal on the roofs
and the kind omen of the moon
shines on the house fronts.

MUSICAL SUBSTITUTE

The last swallows, a black band on the sleeve
of autumn. We will come back — they said.
When and where will they come back? The landscape changes.
Clouds upon clouds gather on the hills.
Then mist, lorries, smoke, timber.
No motorcycles now on the shore road.
Deep calm, a mournful equilibrium, only
the waiting for the big winds and the old women with the rocket leaves.
In the inner room footsteps are heard,
soft footsteps on the ashes. A red pullover thrown on the chair.
                    The day after tomorrow
in the empty rooms the cornet's reveille will sound
among the music-stands of the absent;
the rousing music will fill the intervals of time
and the cornet-player (I should tell you — he said)
will be no-one but me.

THESE

These look sideways, always suspicious.
Their hands locked in their pockets.
They have much to say. They say nothing.
The sky continues within them.
That's why you see them sometimes beneath the moon
alone smiling in front of a closed door.

THE HOUR OF WAITING

A girl on the balcony dark hair unbraided.
A transparent moon in the rosy dusk.
A white butterfly on green. Two cyclists
on the bridge. The grape-gatherers with their horses
wash themselves at the shore. Sweet drowsiness
sweet forgetfulness. Hints of the eternal. A sorrowful statue
gazes far off, waiting for Glafki*
to leave a basket of flowers at his feet.

*In mythology, the daughter of Creon of Corinth, and wife of Jason.

GEORGE VAFOPOULOS

(1903–1996)

GEORGE VAFOPOULOS

from
The offering

THE CALENDAR

Behold, three full years
have passed now since
you were carried up
into heaven.

With reverence I open the little box
of your sweet remembrances.

Scent of holiness,
musk of your martyrdom,
its sacred essence permeating
the cell of my loneliness.

Before your humble remembrances
this holy libation of tears.

See, I take out
your slim thermometer,
stilled
at its cold limits.
See, I touch
with trembling fingers
your poor little comb,
your hair's gentle bridle.

But my tearful gaze,
veiled in a mist of reverence,
rests on the little calendar,
where the eyelid

of your last earthly day
fell deeply asleep.

"The sixteenth day of April
Of Love, Peace, Snow, martyrs."*
The end of your suffering,
the flowering again of mine.

. . . .

With reverence I close up the little box
of your sweet remembrances.
The richness of your poor remembrances
mingles with the poverty
of my wealth of tears.

"Of Love, Peace, Snow, martyrs."

Abide in Love.
Rest in Peace.
Whiter than Snow.

---

*The three female martyrs whose memory is honoured on the 16th of April are Ἀγάπη (Love), Εἰρήνη (Peace) and Χιονία (Snow-like).

GEORGE VAFOPOULOS

from
Songs of resurrection

    THOU IN ME

A pile of ancient books.
Darkened icons on the walls.
On my overloaded table
the vigilant lamp keeps watch,
image of my yearning.

In this lonely dwelling
sleepless I searched for You
through the heavy wintry nights
among the piles of ancient books
and the images of the darkened icons.
But nowhere did I find You.

See, I wrap my heavy cloak
round my bent body.
In my sinewed hand I grasp
the staff of my bitter quests.

See, I leave the cave
of my sterile worldly wisdom.
Painfully I turn my steps
to the air, the sun, and the stars.

I bend down, I ask the flower.
It heard your tread
before the sound of my own footfall
was heard.

I raise my voice
to the bird of heaven.
You had dazzled its sight
before its wing flashed

sword-like through
my own eyes' persistent gaze.

Despairing I invoke
the patient, scrutinizing stars.
The music of their heavenly praise
escorting You softly away
had just faded
in the gentle ethereal distance.

I quicken my pace.
Age-old traveller
gone before.
I place my feet
in the footprints
of your silent steps.

But see,
an insuperable barrier
marks the end
of my untiring march.
Dark, deep, indestructible
the heavy-pounding sea
rears itself before me.

So there comes between us then
the indestructible fury
of the cold tempestuous sea?
The last footprints of your sandals
fade, dissolving slowly
in the pommelling of the waves.

I sit, my spirit watchful
at the sheer and pitiless brink
of the black abyss.
The deep, dark infernal well
of my dolorous fate
gapes before me.

Above me the network of stars
behind me the wall of night

before me the barrier
of the unconquerable sea.

Despair.

Desperate I hurl my voice
at the stars, the night, and the sea.
Am I alone?
"Alone!"
My voice rebounds from the stars, the night, and the sea
in the black infernal well
tumbling and re-echoing.

So you deny me
the yearned-for blessing
of heavenly union?

It has slipped then
from the tips
of my torn fingers
the guiding thread
of the divine long hoped-for touch?

My bloodstained forehead
drops in dejection
to the cold well's edge.
Hollow-eyed
my weary spirit
sinks deep into dormition.

Then behold, in the painful numbness of my soul
You, in all Your glory,
on the wings of the wind
stand upright
there before me
face to face.

Out of the deep, infernal well
of my grievous fate
behold, the message of Your profound,
mysterious, and prophetic voice

floods through my spirit.

The victory hymn
of flowers, birds, and stars
permeates the channels of my soul.

Filled with the sounds of heaven
I spring free of the chains of torpor
And I haul my painful body up
again to the brink of the dark abyss.

I send out my voice in triumph
to the stars, the night, and the sea.
Thou in me.
The brotherly chorus
of flowers, birds, and stars
chants with me "Thou in me"
to the blithely echoing heavens.

Thou in me,
the one besought.

GEORGE VAFOPOULOS

from
The big night and the window

SCALES

On the one scale put the sun;
put the sea; put song.
Pile up all the islands of the Aegean,
with the sea shells of happy poets.
What else remains? Love. Put then,
at the top, above all else, love.

But this pyramid of joy
would be raised vertical
if on the other scale were laid
the merest something from a hospital.

THE HEDGEHOG

I had forgotten you, frightened little creature,
when in my loneliness and silence
invoking the spirit of Helen Keller*
I besought the dog's companionship.

Love and fear were born at the same hour.
And while love pours through your being
like a river within, dividing into many channels,
fear, to protect love's hiding place,
has built a castle on your back: a horde of lancers
keeps sleepless watch at the lookouts, lying in wait.

Leaning over the hedge, I caress you,
unsuspecting little vessel of love.
You do not see, but only sense me.
Or rather, you sense your safety. And so
your lancers have fallen asleep at their posts.

Loneliness helps me to enter your being,
without your knowing it, and I learn the great
lesson of fear: that it protects my love.

My brother, how many times did you lend me
this panoply of yours; how many times
did your quills shoot up on my skin,
when the fear trembling now within me
sought the protection of love.

---

* At age 19 months, Helen Keller (1880–1968) lost both her sight and her hearing. Anne Sullivan Macy (1866–1936) taught her the relationship between words and things. Helen first spoke at age ten. She graduated from Radcliffe College in 1904 and received honorary degrees from universities worldwide.

FEAR

This loneliness and this silence are not
the old loneliness or the old silence. Those are not even
memories any more: they are sunk in the depths of night.
These blossomed around you, like night flowers,
when fear beckoned you to close the window.

Before that, you were standing at its open frame watching
the children playing in the yard below. Yet
you didn't see their movements nor did you hear their voices.
You were only remembering them, because they lay in your past.
And you felt all the children's love reaching up
to your whole being, because love
is beyond time and beyond partition.

Sometimes you saw there where you were seeing nothing.
Sometimes you heard when you were hearing nothing.
And your window suddenly found itself opening
like an astonished eye, high up in this tower,
girded round with a moat of stagnant water.
And you hastened to close the window, before
the subterranean voices from the swamp drowned you.

But you did not suspect you were guarding fear,
that you were keeping all your love closed in.
This loneliness comes of your fear.
Love has sealed the lips of this silence.

GEORGE VAFOPOULOS

from
The sequel

FIRST SYMPHONY
IN RED AND WHITE

In this garden the roses were white
because they wore the raiment of children's voices.
But when the chirruping of infants
was cut short by the roaring panzer's clatter
and the voices, garments, and the little bodies
were ground in its metal teeth
then all the roses in the garden suddenly turned red.

And the sun has turned red too; red
roses have sprouted in the breasts of adolescents.
Red poppies have drowned the fields
in the seed of the "sleep-bearing flower".
And this white bread of ours has reddened,
since clean knives are no longer to be found.

How to discern you, Lord of the world,
in the midst of this red flood,
my eyes covered
with a veil of red tears?

How to hear your deep hidden voice,
since shrieking metal stuns
my hearing? How can I behold your countenance
behind this crimson cataract?

Lord of the world, if by chance you have not moved
to another world among your worlds,
and if by chance red voices can still
sprinkle your hearing with scarlet drops,
I believe your miracles are possible,
not indeed to whiten the soul of the world

but to give it a semblance of whiteness.

Give me then the eyes of happy poets,
whose privilege is to see
only white snowflakes, white-petalled
flowers, white cataracts, and white sheets.

Give me the hands of those delicate princes,
who possess the art of plucking the white
down from your angels' wings
to cover this gaudy
red morass that offends their sight.

Give me their sensitive white hearing,
that catches only the whisper of wings,
because the grinding roar of the panzer
rides beyond their acoustic field.

Give me too their charming white lips,
that, while not disdaining to kiss red lips as well,
whisper only white flowery verses,
clothed in the white muslin of clouds.

But if, Lord, you have indeed migrated
to another world among your many worlds,
or if by chance my drowned voice has not the strength
to shatter this thick red crust
where the soles of my feet have sunk deep,
or if you have lost the power for miracles,
which is now enclosed in a metal fist,
I think that my hands at least could
wash the panzer's metal teeth.

And let me send you, by long-distance missiles,
as souvenirs from the world you have forsaken,
the frozen chirrupings of infants,
with their white garments that now are red,
covering their little crushed bodies.

NIKOS

GATSOS

(1911–1992)

Amorgos

> *Bad witnesses to men are the eyes and*
> *ears of those who have barbarous souls.*
> HERACLITUS

1

Their country lashed to the sails and the oars hanging in the wind
the shipwrecked slept calm as dead wild beasts on a bedding of sponge
but seaweed eyes are turned to the sea
lest the south wind with fresh dyed lateen carry them back
and a lost elephant is always worth much more than the trembling breasts of a girl
only let the roofs of lonely mountain chapels light up with the yearning of the evening star
let birds flutter in the masts of the lemon tree
with the steady white breath of new fledged motion
then will come winds the bodies of swans that stayed immaculate tender and still
among steam-rolling shops and cyclonic vegetable gardens
when women's eyes became coals and the hearts of chestnut sellers broke
when the harvest stopped and the hopes of crickets began.

Therefore young men with wine kisses and leaves in your mouths
I want you to go out naked into rivers
and sing Barbary as the woodsman hunts for the lentisk
as the adder passes through barley fields
with its proud and angry eyes
and as the lightning threshes youth.

And do not laugh do not cry do not rejoice
do not vainly tighten your boots as if you were planting plane trees
do not become FATE
because the golden eagle is not a closed drawer
it is not a tear from the plum tree nor a smile from the water-lily
neither is it in the dove's shirt nor the Sultan's mandoline
nor silk attire for the head of the whale
it is a saw from the sea that cuts seagulls to pieces
it is a carpenter's pillow a beggar's clock

it is a fire in a blacksmith's that scoffs at priests' wives and lulls the lilies to sleep
it is the match-making of Turks and the Australians' feast-day
it is the lair of Hungarians
where in the autumn the hazelnut trees go secretly meeting together
they see the wise storks dyeing their eggs black
and they too weep
they burn their nightgowns and put on the duck's petticoat
spreading stars on the earth for kings to walk upon
with their silver amulets the crown and the purple
they scatter rosemary on the flower beds
for mice to go to another pantry
to go into other churches to eat the Lord's Table
and the owls my children
the owls howl
and dead nuns rise to dance
with tambourines drums and fiddles with pipes and lutes
with pennons and with herbal censers and veils
wearing bears' trousers they eat the ferrets' mushrooms in the frozen valley
they play heads or tails with the ring of Saint John and the gold coins of the Blackamoor
they laugh at witches
they cut a priest's beard with the yataghan of Kolokotronis
they bathe in the vapour from the incense
and then chanting slowly go into the earth again and are silent
as waves are silent as the cuckoo at dawn as the oil-lamp in the evening.

And so in a deep jar the grape dries
in the belfry of a fig tree the apple ripens
so with a gaudy necktie
summer breathes under the tent of the vine
and a tender love of mine sleeps naked among the white cherry trees
a girl unfading as the bough of an almond tree
her head on her raised elbow and her palm on her gold coin
on its morning warmth when quiet as a thief
the dawn star comes through a window of spring to wake her!

2

They say that the mountains shake and the fir trees are angry
when night gnaws at the nails on the slates to let the goblins in

when hell sucks in the frothing toil of the torrents
or when the hairline on the pepper tree is pummelled by the north wind.

Only the oxen of the Achaians in the lush pastures of Thessaly
graze sturdy and strong the eternal sun gazing upon them
they eat the green grass poplar leaves celery they drink clear water in the dykes
they sniff the earth's sweat and then fall heavily under the shade of the willow to sleep.

Cast away the dead said Heraclitus and he saw heaven blench
he saw in the mud two small cyclamen kissing
and he too fell down to kiss his dead body in the hospitable earth
as the wolf comes down from the forests to see the dead dog and to bewail
what use to me is the drop shining on your brow?
I know the thunderbolt wrote its name on your lips
I know the eagle built its nest in your eyes
but here on this watery bank there is one road only
one deceiving road only and you must cross it
you must plunge into blood before time overtakes you
and go across to the other side to find your companions again
flowers birds deer
to find another sea another gentleness
to seize Achilles' horses by the reins
rather than sit mutely rebuking the river
stoning the river as did Kitsos' mother*
because you too will have been lost and your beauty will have aged
in the branches of an ozier I see your childhood shirt drying
take it, a flag of life to shroud death
and may your tear not flow on this implacable earth
as the tear of the penguin flowed once on the frozen waste
complaining does not serve.
Life will be the same everywhere with the serpents' flute in the land of ghosts
with the song of brigands in fragrant woods
with the knife of suffering in the face of hope
with spring pining deep in the screech owl's heart
it is enough for a plough to be found and a sharp sickle in a blithe hand
it is enough for only a little wheat
to ripen for feasts a little wine for memory a little water for the dust . . .

---

*In the Klephtic ballad *Tou Kitsou*, Kitsos' mother, unable to cross to the other side of the river where her son and his fellow brigands are assembled, throws stones at the water in frustration.

3

In the yards of the afflicted the sun does not rise
only worms come up to mock the stars
only horses thrive on ant heaps
and bats eat birds and piss semen.

In the yards of the afflicted night does not fade
only the leaves vomit a river of tears
when the devil comes in to mount the dogs
and ravens swim in a well of blood.

In the yards of the afflicted the eye has run dry
the brain has frozen and the heart has petrified
the flesh of frogs hangs in the spider's teeth
hungry locusts scream at vampire feet.

In the yards of the afflicted black grass grows
only one May evening a wind passed
a light tread like the frisking plain
a kiss from the foam-decked sea.

And if you thirst for water we will squeeze a cloud
and if you hunger for bread we will slaughter a nightingale
only be patient a moment for the healing rue to open
for the black sky to open for the mullein to flower.

But it was a wind that has gone, a lark that has flown
it was the face of May the white of the moon
a light tread like the frisking plain
a kiss from the foam-decked sea.

4

Awake, clear running water from the pine tree root, that you might find the eyes of sparrows and revive them watering the earth with the scent of basil and the whistling of the lizard. I know you are a naked vein beneath the wind's fearful gaze a mute spark amid the shining crowd of stars. No one sees you no one stops to listen to your breath but you with heavy tread through proud nature will one day reach the leaves of the apricot tree will climb on the supple body of the young broom bush and roll from the eyes of a lover like an adolescent moon. There is an immortal stone that a passing human angel once wrote his name upon and a song that no one yet knows neither the wildest children nor the wisest nightingales. The stone is now closed up in a cave on Mount Devi in the valleys and ravines of my native land but when the cave opens sometime and this angelic song leaps forth against decay and time the rain will suddenly stop and the mud will dry the snow will melt in the mountains the wind will sing the swallows will come to life again the osiers will quiver and when the people with cold eyes and pale faces hear the bells ringing by themselves in the cracked bell towers they will find festive hats to wear and proud tassels to tie on their shoes. Because then no one will jest any more the blood in the streams will overflow animals will break their bridles in the stalls the hay will turn green in the stables the fresh poppies and may flowers will spring up on roof tiles and at all the crossroads they will light red fires at midnight. Then timid girls will quietly come to throw their last garment into the fire and they will dance naked around it exactly like the time we too were young and a window will open at dawn so that in their breasts a flaming carnation might sprout. Perhaps children remembrance of ancestors is a deeper solace and more precious company than a handful of rosewater and the intoxication of beauty no different from the sleeping rosebush of the Evrotas. Goodnight then I see a host of falling stars rocking your dream but I hold in my fingers the music for a better day. Travellers from India can tell you more than all the Byzantine Chroniclers.

5

During the course of his mysterious life man
has bequeathed to his descendants multifarious and worthy tokens of his immortal
        lineage
as he has also bequeathed traces of ruins of dawn avalanches of celestial reptiles as
        well as kites, diamonds, and glances of hyacinths
in the midst of sighs tears hunger lamentation and the ashes of underground wells.

6

How very much I loved you I alone know
I who once touched you with the eyes of the Pleiades
and with the mane of the moon I embraced you and we danced on the summer plains
on the gathered reeds and we ate together the cut clover
great black sea with so many pebbles round your neck so many coloured gems in your hair.

A ship comes into shore a rusty well-wheel groans
a plume of blue smoke on the rosy horizon
like the rending wing of the crane
armies of swallows wait to say their welcome to the brave
arms rise naked tattooed with anchors
children's cries mingle with the west wind singing
bees go in and out of cows' nostrils
Kalamatan kerchiefs wave
and a distant bell dyes the sky blue
like the sound of a church bell travelling in the stars
so many centuries gone
from the soul of the Goths and from the domes of Baltimore
and from the great lost monastery of Aya Sofya.
But who are these on the high mountain gazing
with calm eye and serene countenance?
This dust in the air is the echo of what conflagration?
Is it Kalyvas fighting or Levendoyannis?*
Have the Germans joined battle with the Maniates?
Neither Kalyvas is fighting nor Levendoyannis
nor have the Germans joined battle with the Maniates.
Silent towers guard a phantom princess
cypress tops befriend a dead anemone
peaceful shepherds sing their morning song with a lime-tree reed
a foolish hunter fires a shot at turtle doves
and an old forgotten windmill
with a dolphin's needle mends its rotting sails
and comes down from the slopes with a favouring north-west wind

---

*Kalyvas and Levendoyannis (properly called Bakoyannis) were chieftains who fought for Geek independence. Referred to in the historical ballad *Tou Diakou (24 April 1821)*.

as Adonis descended the footpaths of Chelmos to say good evening to Golfo.*

My tormented heart year after year I strove with ink and hammer
with fire and gold to make you an embroidery
a hyacinth from an orange tree
a flowering quince tree to console you
I who once touched you with the eyes of the Pleiades
and with the mane of the moon I embraced you and we danced on the summer plains
on the gathered reeds and we ate together the cut clover.
Vast black solitude with so many pebbles round your neck so many coloured gems in
        your hair.

*The heroine of a popular play written in 1894 by Spyros Peresiades, Golfo is a shepherdess who goes insane when abandoned by her lover.

from
Lend silken threads to the wind

*Since I have been mourning
my golden and blue
and heavenly light
the rhythm of the world
has changed within me*
          G. VIZYINOS

SPANISH RHAPSODY

In memory of Ravel

Bare trees. Bare trees.
Plains of stone. Mute villages.
I will embroider the wilderness
with vineyards and bell-towers.
Bare trees. Bare trees.
Yellow earth. Dim mountains.
Malaga and Monemvasia.
Bring wine to inspire me.
Bare trees. Bare trees.
Once at a river two willows sprang
a child crying for joy embalmed in the roots.
Put your ear to the earth.
And hear clearly its breathing
as the seagull hears
when it sleeps on the sand
the lament of the sea.

Bare trees. Bare trees.
Once in a sky two doves flew

lean black horsemen held their steeds for a moment
the reins tremble in their hands, the prickly pears gaze at them.
Frightened clouds gather in the distance.

— ◆ —

To bring you herbs and myrrh
jewels of the earth that you will plant
in the frost of wearied thoughts
in the salt of tearful bitterness,

alone I took the road one evening
that leads to the flowering slopes.
. . . .

— ◆ —

What can you say? Virgins stoop
and the colours of the orange tree do not change in winter
and the stars that sink in the north motionless
tearful numberless do not shed their ashes.
What can you give? Take your turn
lend silken threads to the wind and if it covers the sea calm your soul
the lightning did not fall on the dry leaves in spring
anemones did not roll under the feet of women without mercy
even here in the poplars the dew came like a hunted bird and had no time
to whisper her prayer.

— ◆ —

TAKE YOUR RING

To the memory of Maria Nomikou

God will have smiled once at the fire in your eye
Spring will have closed her heart like a pearl on an ancient shore.
Now as you sleep shining
on the sands of the stars, a tear of the Pleiades
a sharp pebble
in the arms of Celaeno and Maia.*
Take your ring
take silver from the meadows to paint your brow
and come to me and sleep
sinking eternally into a springlike sea
on a summer night when I will speak to your eyes
lost on the shores of some pale Galaxy.
Come like April sun to the window of my dreams
wearing a ribbon round your neck
to greet the cranes travelling to strange lands
to close a rose as the doves lull a child to sleep
beneath the leaves in the vineyards on the slope of the White River
in the arms of plane trees at a cave of the Evrotas.

For you life was like a tear from the sea
like a summer fire and a kerchief of May
as you too were a deep blue wave of hers
a bitter pebble of hers
a little swallow of hers roaming the woods
without fire for the dawn without stars in spring
your warm heart turned toward strange lands
to the broken teeth of the other shore
to the dead children of the wild cherry tree and the seal.

*Two of the seven daughters of Atlas and Pleione. According to mythology, the hunter Orion fell in love with them and pursued them through the woods until Zeus, in order to save them, transformed them into stars, forming the constellation of the Pleiades.

Beat tambourines on the slopes. In this gorge
near the bitter almond trees Federico sleeps
his eyes starry his soul an abyss.
Tell the horses to stop
tell the children not to run
tell the rivers to be silent
lest they grieve his heart.

— ◆ —

Patient horses wait in the courtyard.
Who will tell them of green rivers
and who will saddle them at dawn?

He who loved them . . .
. . . .
. . . .
Dead centuries of the moon since
. . . .

— ◆ —

ORANGE TREE OF AEGINA

From the light of the golden beach in your eyes
a wing gathers its shade
a wind strives with the south wind.

I wonder what hand will put on you
a handful of soil from the Morea?
Little mother orange tree
throw the orange to your earth
. . . .
. . . . an embrace
love, the broad sea

— ◆ —

    Blood, blood, blood,
    desire iron smoke
    roses withered clocks stopped
    a big ox hangs among the jasmine.

— ◆ —

Down in the white sea
I shall sleep the sleep of children
the stake of an apple-tree I planted last year
will be orange blossom in your hair
only do not tell your shadow to come.

— ◆ —

Because I took you
from your dark lair and brought you up to the clouds
to see the golden eagles in their eyries and dancers on threshing floors
to see crosses in lonely chapels and stars on the roofs of trees
to see a thoughtful love on the balconies of the moon
and then with your tear and your smile
to gaze on me as in a dream and take my hand
with the ribbon round your neck to greet the cranes
with your blond hair to mock the sun
with your naked breasts to laugh at the lilies
with the blue of your eyes to challenge the sky.

— ◆ —

A SUMMER NIGHT

To Andreas Embirikos

Merope I close my eyes to remember the earth that absorbed the blood of slaughtered birds in its entrails and became somewhere fire smoke and iron beyond the dust of rivers where the willows sing. On the evening mountains a star sparkles wanting to start the chorus of the swallows and the crickets.

— ◆ —

    Ah, what a withered meadow!
    Door closed to beauty!
    I seek for a child
               to heal my grief
    with dahlias from the sleeping moon.

— ◆ —

A ruined bell-tower
shows the road of fire to the shipwrecked
it tells the fate of reptiles to the dead
perhaps the sea will change but the spring does not change
perhaps the clouds will dissolve but your memory will not dissolve
perhaps heroes will weep but the emerald does not weep
copper is not seduced by two grapes.

───◆───

NIKIFOROS

VRETTAKOS

(1912–1991)

from
Gifts in abeyance

EUPHORIA

This evening my soul ascended, a full moon
rising. And I said: I do not see an end.
It seems that evermore these hands of mine
will caress the young leaves on the trees
will gather the light, will sketch it.
They will give themselves.
                              Dawn awakening,
I climb higher. I gaze
at the horizon. I do not see an end.

WHATEVER HAPPENS

Whatever happens, I will not deny
the world. And if they cut off my hands
and I cannot clasp them, I shall be able
to lean my forehead on the tree
my forehead on the stone, my cheek
worn by solitude on the light.

SHORT ODE

Sitting opposite my gracious
mountain, I consider and reflect. Our world
an exquisite chain of colours,
of things. Perfection and light.
And I say that it must not be
inhabited by hate in arms
but be a garden, the marvellous
church of the created universe.
And only visitors from other
planets, bare of beauty,
should come in to worship.

TREE PLANTING

Words are the tree on which
my soul branches out and turns into flowers
that will bloom forever. Fruits
for the hungering who have not yet
been born.
        I feel joy
that I planted almond trees, pear trees
but also other trees, like
these short poems of mine.

THE GREEK LANGUAGE

When I sometime leave this light
I shall meander upwards like a
murmuring stream.
And if by chance somewhere among
the azure corridors
I meet with angels, I shall speak
to them in Greek, since
they do not know languages. They
speak among themselves with music.

THE FIELD OF WORDS

Like the bee round a wild
flower, so am I. I prowl
continuously around the word.

I thank the long lines
of ancestors who moulded the voice.
Cutting it into links, they made
meanings. Like smelters they
forged it into gold and it became
Homer, Aeschylus, the Gospels
and other jewels.
      With the thread
of words, this gold
from gold, which comes from the depths
of my heart, I am linked, I take part in
the world.
    Consider:
I said and wrote, "I love."

THE TEN COMMANDMENTS

I minister to the pain of life, but I must
not forget that I was also born
a priest of beauty and I ought to
celebrate our world, to make a
scripture of its radiance.
       First
and Tenth Commandment
of beauty: love.

THE EYES OF INSECTS

I often try to fathom the depth
of insects' eyes. All together
they would form above us a
starlit, flowing, lower
sky. It is wonderful to know
how many sun-filled worlds, cleverly
wrought, compose our world.

THE TULIP

He who will come in the night may
be Jesus. Or his first
cousin. It may be his mother's
youngest sister or his father.
Or maybe a villager soaked by the rain,
overtaken by night. There's always a bed left over.
God has paid the rent for me,
planting within me a
white tulip: Love.

THE DECAY OF HANDS

What has become of those hands that made
stone into beauty, walls
into angels, colours into a stream of light
extending earth to heaven,
heaven to earth?

MEMORY OF LOST BLOOD

And those who have been killed for the dream
that remained a dream, frequently setting off,
for no reason, from the ends
of time, visit me.

They swarm in the garden, in my surrounding
hills. A shadow hides the moon.

They thin away, then dissolve, like
the waters of a great flood
receding.
      (That we might become
all together one person, a Jesus
who in the icon facing me
weeps for his blood.)

OUT OF SUPERFLUITY

The plan was greater, Lord.
But I accomplished only
what time and earning my bread
allowed me. I did not beg,
I had no need. Because even nakedness, when
one believes in the light, is
a garment. And even from a crumb
you can have a superfluity.
And nothing is not nothing,
Lord. You will see. When I come
to you I will bring you flowers.

NIKIFOROS VRETTAKOS

from
Chorus

THE CLOUD

It is not the cloud that today,
the fifth of May, at six in the evening,
gilded the horizon.
It is my love
that broke through the boundaries
of my heart and enveloped
the whole world
in a diaphanous garland.

FOURTEEN POEMS
FOR THE SAME MOUNTAIN

I

Not yet have I come to say farewell
to you my brother, whom I climbed
for the first time when I was a light
on a stem. Most of my
verses are buildings
on you. And if my words
became the Word, we would stay upright
then the two of us like parallel
stones. But within
the jumbled forest of the world
today the Word is hardly
heard. Yet I know that from
my books tomorrow children
will gather flowers and they will talk
of the miracle-life, gazing at
the world through my verses.

II
I climbed you up and down, carrying
the sky for my needs.
My words, flower cups, had to fill
with light. My verses
flower pots in God's window.

III
When I came into the world and saw
the sun, I said: I will have to leave
something behind me departing.

And this was enough: to climb up
to your peak, and throw
a flower to the earth.

IV
I saw the lightning, its snake-like
quiver. Wavering in the air
it lit your peak from
bottom to top. And a thought played
in my skull like a lightning flash:
jumping on the first step I could climb
one by one, from bottom to top
its slanting stair.

V

The heavenly lace of your outlines
undulating almost —
you would think that
when the sun sets
it fills with angels.

They advance climbing
from the two ridges
up to your mighty peak.

They come together upon it
like a chorus.

Until at last
one of them
stretches out his hand
and lights the evening star.

VI

Up here death is unknown
I sometimes said and wrote. And it was
true. It often happened.
The ravines would close.
The cold wind and shades
of night found no
passage.

The light outside and inside me
       would meet
and spread boundless around me.

VII

I was ten years old when I carved
my name with a penknife
on your slate, for the rising sun
to spell out its letters. It was then
that I still had "I", but later
I erased it, as
did the rain my name
from your slate.
                  My name
the voice of a nightingale
that comes from the forest
without my name.
It is enough for me to know that
the light of words drips
God into the souls of children.

VIII

I promised the one who was all things.
I smiled at the one who was all things.
You were not the one, my good mountain.
I gave you a face. I saw you as a people
and I saw you as a planet. And I had
a beautiful dream: that smiling thus
upon you I could change
all the clouds into the sun's fringe
a hurricane into phosphorescence of peace.

IX

I needed you to exist. To find
somewhere to rest my grief.
At times when everything, people,
feelings, ideas, were shifting
I needed a solid stone
to lay my papers on.

Do not take away your stone,
Lord, and leave my hands
in the void. I have more to write.

X

I have travelled struggling through many
winds that found my breast
exposed and froze me. Guttering
thunderbolts corroded my brow
and now we stand
one facing the other
like two gray brother
rocks.
      But your peace
always my peace.
Sitting at your feet
covered with wounds, I bless
existence.
      Out of all the great
riches that I hymn, fate
has allowed that I
too have a stone in the universe.

XI

It tried hard this rough
weather, but in the end
did not lay waste my soul
which stayed here standing
beside you, to dress you,
at the time of joyful days, and
tidings.
        This will be your
festive robe.

XII

I want to weave, render in words
the rhythm of the water, beating
on the stones beneath your ferns.
That my soul too may be heard
rolling along, word by word, in
my verses, that it may flow
unceasing, clear, tender
(heaven on either side)
as chamber music flows through time.

XIII

I spoke to you with the words of the shepherds
that I guarded in my blood. The words
were naked and my blood dressed them in a garment
to match my discourse
with the world — with all creatures and things.
Together they form a river
of beauty, that right here,
between us two and around us
cuts through the abyss in the length and
breadth of this earth.

XIV

I know that you were before
I was born. Yet your
height came from within me.

CREATION

I reckon I have still a thousand
poems to write. I am going to buy
paper for six days. And I wonder:
with how many thousand poems
did the Lord make his sun?

THE WORKSHOP

I do not know where
the poems come from
which like doves
one behind the other
flutter from within me.
I do not know where
the messages come from.

(There is a place
within me, where
belts revolve
pistons move
things happen
I don't exactly know.)

Love and pain
work ceaselessly.

POETRY

Poetry is: God
who marches
towards all the world
with his hands open.

EPIGRAM OF LIFE

Every day I see him, as if for the first
time, rising from sea or mountain.
Always new-created, he grows
ushering into our life his spreading
river. Rarely it happens
that I do not catch him, but even then
I hear him rolling golden in my sleep.

CHORUS

Church lit to its depths
above me, this evening,
the universe anew. And I
born at its extreme point
was able, alone, uncovered
and barefoot to present myself.
And I became its cantor.

I lean my shoulder against the trunk
on one side of a tree
(on the other a cricket
at the top a nightingale) and the light
streams unceasing from my lips.

NEITHER

Neither loneliness nor the night
hold fear for me. I am
well, I live without want.
I have found the breasts
with the milk of the universe.

PASCHAL EXALTATION

The sky blows golden light
into things. I know it
from my own heart
where colours
chase one another, a thousand Castalian* fountains
chant and an Evrotas.°

The Lord tamed and bound
his tempests
over the abyss. And so it was
Easter. And I do not know
if the world has given its peace
to me, or if I have given it
my peace. Even these
mountains surrounding me
that were always love,
gentle and soft
cannot in this diaphanous
boundless day hide
their movements.

They march in the sky.

---

*An ancient name for a fountain near Delphi, today called Aiyannis.
°A river in Laconia, near Sparta.

MILTOS

SACHTOURIS

(1919–2005)

from
The forgotten woman

THE DREAM

> *Notre voyage à nous est entièrement
> imaginaire. Voilà sa force.*
> L. F. Céline

The eternal dream
caresses its white hair

Youths undress in the light
throw the ball and shout in triumph
a Catholic priest points to Lykavitos
a naked youth smiles at the girls
they grow tall in their branches they shout
he's lame he's lame
then ashamed they plunge into the red water

Young women undress in the shade
frightened at the endless harbour
a surgeon on the balcony plays with his lancets
tired dockers are on the watch
to cut the ship's cables
to tear the virginal dresses in shreds
to mutiny and hang the captain
on the big mast in the sky
for women to clench their fingers
close their eyes and sigh
show their teeth their tongues

The journey of joy begins

The suffering woman undressed in the dark
clambered up the wretched house and
stopped the hollow music

she laughed in the mirror lifted her hands
painted her face with the colour
of an expectation saw the sun
in her watch then remembered:
   — You see the poem has come true
   the illegitimate boy and the colour
   give joy
   but how will they photograph this place
   it is the land of hypocrisy
   it is the country where children
   who have lost their innocence lie in wait
   and stretch out their hands at the open windows
   so that sick kisses fall
   so that young short-lived orphans
   fall crying from the windows
   clutching in their wounded hands
   a tuft of white hair

From the ancient dream

BEAUTY

He sprinkled ugliness with beauty
he took a guitar
he walked beside a river
singing

He lost his voice
the frenzied woman stole it
who cut off her head in the crimson waters
the poor man has no longer a voice to sing with
and the river rolls the serene head
with its eyelids closed

Singing

THE THREE LOVERS

On the wet streets of evening
a hazy blue light rises
broad hand on heart
ruined footsteps
three lovers pass hand in hand
        the first

Hangs his love on a tree
at midnight he prays beneath the tree
for his love clinging to the leaves to come down
for the flood of melting leaves to cease
a dog drinks up his tears on the ground
his love in the branches stones him
the tree howls the wind the dog
        the second

Gave his love to a mad violinist
the madman made up a song about her
the sky rains flowers coins
the streets echo to the baleful violin
all have now learned the song of love
with blue lips pursed they whistle it
he alone does not know it
        the third

Made a boat from his love
he launched it on the three seas
he has become a child again
he builds sandcastles
gathers pebbles and shells
and waits for his boat
his love to return

All three have carved a tree on their hearts
a violin at their ear will drive them mad
and on the seabed the captain plays with coral

from
Ballads

THE DEAD MAN IN OUR LIVES
IOANNIS VENIAMIN D'ARKOZI

To Nikos Engonopoulos

Ioannis Veniamin d'Arkozi, who died —
"in the midst of life" — and revived, as soon as night falls
each evening slaughters his herds — goats oxen
and many sheep — strangles all his birds and empties
his rivers and on the black cross
he has set up in the middle of his room
he crucifies his loved one. Then he sits before
the open window poor and tearful
smoking his pipe and wishing that
he too had herds of oxen and goats and many sheep
he too had rivers with swift clear water
he too could admire the fluttering of birds
could enjoy the warm breath of woman.

OBSERVATORY

Thieves of the sun
they never once saw a green bough
they never touched a burning mouth
they don't know what colour the sky is

Closed up in dark rooms
they don't know if they will die
they watch
with black masks and heavy telescopes
with the stars in their pocket soiled with crumbs
with the stones of cowards in their hands
they watch on other planets for the light

Let them die

Let every Spring be judged by its joy
every flower by its colour
every hand by its caress
every kiss by its tremor

THE NIGHTMARE

Her name was Seashore and Sunday. She had black eyes black hair black gowns black petticoats and a pitch-black horse. But they called her Seashore and Sunday. Her house was on an island and it was full of pistols crimson robes flags stars in nets machine-guns diving-suits fish-hooks boxes of dreams boxes of bullets island dresses lamps with coloured glass-chimneys coloured head-scarves and an old rusty cannon. When night fell she would light a lantern at the window. It would flare and die flare and die immediately a decrepit boat would moor beside the iron door of the house and one by one five men would slip into the house. Then from a small secret door hidden by agave plants* the First man would come out dead. The Second his face covered with blood holding a most beautiful infant in his arms. The Third also covered with blood holding an automatic tightly in his arms. The Fourth dragging himself along wrapped from head to toe in a heavy dark green cloth. The Fifth also dead. But the most wonderfully dead person was the girl in her pure-white dress stretched out on the floor in the middle of the room beside her slaughtered black horse. She too soaked in blood her hands crossed high on her breast and smiling with a green twig in her mouth while the five Germans powerless before her stood to attention and saluted her.

---

* The Greek name of the agave is *athanata* which means "immortal". The agave plant lives for many years and when it dies it is perpetuated by suckers at its base. It is also called "the century plant" because of its longevity.

THE GIFTS

Today I put on a
warm red blood
today people love me
a woman smiled at me
a girl gave me a shell
a boy gave me a hammer

Today I kneel on the pavement
I nail the bare white feet of the passers-by
to the paving stones
they are all in tears
but no-one is frightened
they all stay in the places
where I caught them
they are all in tears
but they gaze at the heavenly advertisements
and a beggar woman selling hot cross buns
in the sky

Two people whisper
what's he doing is he nailing our hearts?
yes he's nailing our hearts
so then he's a poet

DEEP MINE

With fear I write to you from an all-night arcade
lit by a tiny lamp like a thimble
a wagon carefully passes above me
edging forward so as not to hit me
while I sometimes pretend I'm asleep other times
that I'm darning a pair of old socks
because everything around me has strangely deteriorated

In the house
yesterday
as I opened the wardrobe it vanished and turned into
dust and all its clothing too
the plates break as soon as you touch them
I'm afraid and I've hidden the knives and forks
my hair has become something like oakum
my mouth has gone white and hurts me
my hands are stone
my feet are wood
three small children are round me crying
I don't know how it happened and they're calling me mother

I wanted to write to you about our old happiness
but I have forgotten how to write about happy things

Remember me

THE SKY

Birds black arrows of intractable grief
it's not easy for you to love the sky
you've learned well to say that it's blue
do you know its caves its forests its rocks?
as you pass thus like winged whistles
you tear your flesh on its window-panes
your downy feathers stick to its heart

And when night comes with fear from the trees
you gaze at the sky's white kerchief the moon
at the naked virgin howling in its lap
the old woman's mouth with its rotten teeth
the stars with swords and golden strings
the lightning the thunderbolt the rain
the distant erotic bliss of its galaxy

SOMETIMES THE WOMEN

Sometimes a bird comes out of the cloud
it passes above the houses and comes down to the city
for years once it was imprisoned in the moon
and that is why it is very bitter very bright
with only one large beautiful eye like the eye of a woman

Out of the cloud it comes down with the rain
passing like a phantom above the houses
on the streets they call out to it bird bird of the rain
it doesn't stop anywhere because if it stops
a thousand scattered fingers will point to it
because it's a cruel bird that's been dyed in blood
an angry bird that comes down with rain to the city
and it has a very beautiful eye like the eye of a woman

That's why women are disturbed when they see it
but some hide it in their mirrors
some hide it in deep drawers
and others deep in their bodies
so it can't be seen
the men don't see it who caress them in the evening
nor in the morning dressing in front of the mirror
do they see it
because it's a very bitter very bright
very frightened bird

IT ISN'T OEDIPUS

A big sky filled with swallows
enormous halls doric columns
hungry ghosts
sitting on chairs in corners
bewailing
rooms with dead bodies
Aegistus the net Kostas
Kostas the grief-stricken fisherman
a room full of multi-coloured tulle undulating
bitter oranges break the window-panes
and in come
Kostas slaughtered
Orestes slaughtered
Alexis slaugthered
they break the chains on the windows
and in come
Kostas Orestes Alexis
others return to the streets from the fiesta
with lights with banners with trees
they call on Mary to come down
they call on Mary to come down from heaven
Achilles' horses fly in the sky
rockets escort them on their flight
the sun rolls down from hill to hill
and the moon is a green lantern
filled with alcohol
then silence darkens the streets
and the blind man comes out with his cane
children follow him on tip-toe
it isn't Oedipus
it's Ilias from the vegetable market
he plays an exhausting ominous flute
it's the dead Ilias from the vegetable market

from
With face to the wall

ON THE NATURE OF THE BEAST

Don't go away beast
beast with the iron teeth
I'll build you a wooden house
I'll give you an earthen jug
I'll also give you a spear
and I'll give you more blood to amuse you

I'll bring you to other harbours
to see how ships devour their anchors
how masks break in two
and flags are suddenly dyed black

I'll find again for you the same girl
tied up trembling in the dark at night
I'll find again for you the broken balcony
the dog-of-a-sky that kept its rain in a well

I'll find again for you the same soldiers
the one who vanished three years ago
with a hole above his eye
and the one who knocked on doors at night
with his hand cut off

I'll find again for you the rotten apple

Don't go away beast
beast with the iron teeth

EXPERIMENTS FOR
THE REPETITION OF NIGHT

My friends are leaving
they've come to say goodbye

I'll not see my friends again

one is leaving for the next room
his face has turned black
he has put on a dark green cloth
night has fallen
he no longer speaks

another is leaving for the other room
to find the pins
but first he hid behind the curtains
then became frightened
and climbed on the window
to sleep

another took off his shoes
with trembling hands
he took the warm
statue
he brought it into the bedroom
he doesn't know how to set it up

my friends have gone far away
I'll not see them again
my friends

THE SCENE

On the table they had placed
a head of clay
the walls they had decorated
with flowers
on the bed they had cut out of paper
two erotic bodies
on the floor wandered snakes
and butterflies
a big dog kept guard
in the corner

Strings stretched across from all
sides
one would not have been wise
to pull them
one of the strings was urging the bodies
to make love

The unhappiness outside
clawed at the doors

NOSTALGIA RETURNS

The woman undressed and lay on the bed
a kiss opened and closed on the floor
savage forms with knives began to appear on the ceiling
a bird hung on a wall choked and expired
a candle tilted and fell from the candlestick
outside there were cries and trampling of feet

The windows opened a hand came in
then in came the moon
it embraced the woman and they slept together

All night a voice could be heard

The days pass
the snow remains

THE TELEPHONE

We're phoning
about a dead man
where can we find him?
His name?
they reply
He has no name
he's dead
we're searching
the drawers
They've hidden him
They've chased him away
They've saved him
we can't find him
he's dead
they say run out
in the rain and find him
we run out
and we can't find him
I telephone
they say to me — He's gone
they're lying of course
with my big
crimson eye
I see HER
Let's go somewhere else
go about
and ask
They don't know her
They don't know his name
They've forgotten him
I telephone
they say: No
They don't know who I am
They don't know my name
They've forgotten me

I'm dead

THE CARNIVAL

Far away in another world this carnival took place
the little hobby-horse wandered in the deserted streets
where not a soul breathed
dead children climbing up to the sky
they would come down for a moment
to get the paper kites they had forgotten
snow fell glass confetti
bleeding the heart
a woman kneeling
rolled up her eyes as if she were dead
only columns of soldiers passed right–left
right–left with frozen teeth

At night the moon came out
a carnival moon
full of hate
they tied it up and threw it into the sea
having stabbed it

Far away in another world this carnival took place

METAMORPHOSIS

One day I'll awake
as a star
as you said I would
I'll wash the blood
from my hands
and I'll throw away the nails
from my breast
I'll no longer fear the thunderbolt
I'll no longer fear the slaughtered
rooster
one day I'll awake
as a star
as you said I would
then
you'll be a bird
perhaps you'll be a peacock
and I
shall have acquitted myself

YANNIS

KONDOS

(1943–1996)

from
At the coming of day

AN END TO JOURNEYS

I return to your old house.
The dog at the door recognizes me,
a fire burns in your hearth
and smoke rises from the chimney.
The landscape hasn't changed much.
Only the tower opposite
has crumbled. From there at nights
I would follow you with thirsty eyes.
The trees have grown
and some are gone,
for the big road to be opened,
the one I'm walking on now.
Wolves, foxes, and jackals
run round me, tame
as always. Some downy feathers
fall from the sky
— perhaps it's snowing.
The palm tree where you would lean
your back bends now
a little towards the left, from desiring you
to repeat that movement.
Some stones recognized me
and rolled towards me.
The hollow of my eye
saw all this and other things
it remembered and the saliva
of desire became honey.

TWENTY-FOUR-HOUR NEWS

One Anna brought me your news.
You've changed, become blond. You've put an end
to your old habits.
You don't open the door with your palm,
but with your ring-finger.
The garden in front of the house
trampled, as if it awoke
from a toilsome sleep.
The lines of your face broken
by the pressure of kisses.
Coffees everywhere steaming
like volcanoes, and you ready
to fall in. What I wrote
about you, you've hung
on the walls, hides of wild animals
that presume big hunts
for years. Only the afternoon
beguiles you yet and you gaze
at the light, shadows, footprints,
fantasies and the whistling of the young man
in the block of flats opposite.
The short, the long, the lost hours
you convert into needles and sew
balloons, nights, and lies.

MISTAKEN IDENTITIES

Two girls gazed at me
earnestly and spoke to me
in dense epithets.
They were wearing white hats
and flowers flew
from their mouths
as in Botticelli's painting.
I drew the chair
towards them
and the noise could be heard
as far as England.
Because they were English
with red hair
with freckles on their backs
and they were as if drowned
in the water, motionless, beautiful.
But as I was shouting
"Eh . . . what's happening down there?"
they stretched out their small hands
and swept me into the watery silence
probably thinking I was
Edgar Allan Poe.

THE ANATOMIST

"I don't fear time"
said the butcher to me
cutting, mincing, hanging.

"There's no question of going to heaven.
Here I'll stay, humbly, for ever."
He looked at me wiping
the blood-stained hands
on the white apron.

"My house is near the lake.
All night I fish for
eels and moons."

He gives a stab
— straight as silence —
and empties the belly of the lamb.

"In the afternoons, when it rains,
I paint the same landscape."
He separates livers from entrails.

"And I read poems.
Once I read Hölderlin."
The heart slipped from him off the bench.
He bent down, took it and hung it
with the others.

THE TRAVELLER
WITH THE BLACK BOX

That white face,
dyed with white lead,
like a moon, like a shoe,
comes from afar.
He has trodden roads upon roads
to reach these parts.
he has trodden poems
forests and seas
to come to us.

His dark eyes,
billiard balls.
Time, a billiard cue
its end the concrete
moment, and the game is played
everywhere with success.

And as the light falls
softly on the lemon trees, we
eat chocolates laughing
and knowing what awaits us.

from
The nothing athlete

IT COULD BE A BERGMAN FILM

Morning, twilight.
A couple having breakfast.
They gaze indifferent at the steam rising from their tea.

Noon, twilight.
Winter and work.
The house waits breathing nervously.

Afternoon, twilight.
A little stroll around the office.
Their eyes see dim pictures
of yesterday — they see them as happy.

Evening, few words and twilight.
On the same chairs, gazing in front of them,
it is supposed at the lake and the ducks.
They say something about the prime minister,
the increase in production, communications.
Absence instead of water runs
in the veins of the central heating
while their veins freeze.
They wrap themselves in the twilight
and sleep.

BRONZE AGE

The excavations showed your inauspicious
mornings. The earth held the footprints.
When counted there were five men. One of them,
the strongest, was wearing gold sandals.
He it was who broke the door, and the women
scattered. You had just put your foot
into the cistern for the first bath of the day.
Your cries and the steam
are still on the walls.
Everything else has gone:
the oaths, the attempts at explanation,
the entreaties of the nurse,
the terrified flight of the dove.
They found the knives, the blood,
the hair in his hands, your groans,
the rumble and the shards of the earthquake
that occurred at the moment you were murdered.
After thousands of years,
the classifications, the tarnished mirrors, the conservationists,
the museum, the passers-by.

ABSENTMINDED WITH LOVE
OR
WHAT DOES EMILY DICKINSON
WANT OF US?

Put the wings — your blades —
in their sheaths and come let's talk
like human beings. Don't stretch
the bow of your age, you will break it.
It smells of music. With a different eye I see now
the quicksilver of your voice.
All night I was cutting firewood, I was cutting words
in my sleep. I was making monologues,
and the sleet of the poem
bored holes in my bones and I was freezing.
All night I was going down to the basement
where I hide the moon so that I can see
your body. See the fires
of Saint Yannis and Saint Ioannis* himself
with his severed head
in his hand. A stream flows, Emily Dickinson
lifts her skirts and prepares
to cross it. She smiles, gazing with lowered
eyes at the future. Your dog sees nothing
of all this. Playing he pulls the sky
through the streets. Stumbling
I bump into the corners of pictures
to produce sounds, star-dust
and blood of fantasy, in this country
of fear and the final silence.

---

*Both names refer to John the Baptist. Yannis is the more familiar name. To celebrate Saint Yannis's day, fires are lit in Greek villages. Ioannis is the more formal name of the saint.

PEDAGOGICS

You must wash your hands.
You must eat up your food.
You must do your homework.
You must love animals.
You must kill people every day.
You must look ahead to tomorrow and not
at yesterday, because you might be a musician.
You must take promotion with your sword
and your cleverness.
You must not waste time.
You must save.
You must hide your thoughts.
You must be serious (laughter is injurious).
You must be careful at crossroads.

(And call in with me sometime
for a game of chess — said the gentleman
in the black cloak.)

RURAL COUNTRY

I gaze at nature. I am not calm.
I become fierce. I grow thick fur.
I grunt. I sniff the air.
The wolf comes out from inside me.
Nails appear.
I see the moon with loathing.
The music of the leaves
and the music of the water
(of Hegel) make me feel
strange and gray.
I eat my little lamb. I eat
the story of Little Red Riding Hood.
Everything around me goes red.
In so many years I've learned nothing.
Civilization hasn't touched me.
Is love enough? Is this bitch of a life
that has stuck in my throat enough?
I don't know. And this year I let myself go
in the woods and mixed with the pack.
I think again of you, with how much care
you will wipe the blood from my mouth
when I come back home after the hunt.

FOR SCHOOLFELLOWS

Your snows were false
my friends. They melted at first glance.
The terrible skull of the earth appeared.
But the trees, at the same time
have leaves and fruit.
We are warm, we open
our shirts and laugh.
We are warm, we go to the wells,
with ropes we draw up our childhood
words. They are fresh and drinkable yet.
Others play now on the building site.
Our stones and the signs of us
are well-hidden in the ground.

WHAT BECAME OF CHARLES DICKENS'S CHILDREN

They're temporarily lost, they've become shadows,
they follow me for an instant
out of the fog
catching at the hem of my coat.
For them it is a hard winter with snow.
Their shoes worn out, their feelings
in shreds they wander aimlessly about the streets
beneath nineteenth-century lamps.
The snow whistles and beats them mercilessly.
It tries to erase them from the leaves
of books. But they persist in wandering
in our memory, tormenting us, accompanying us.
Pale and hungry they wait for us
at the corner, their shoulders thirsting
for a caress. At dusk we saw them for the first
time and they brought us the most audacious drawings.
There where the music fades the children hide
frightened gazing at the moon.

MARJORIE CHAMBERS

THREE ESSAYS

ON RITSOS

RITSOS AND GREEK MYTHOLOGY

MARJORIE CHAMBERS

This essay was first published in *Hermathena: A Trinity College Dublin Review*, No. CLIII, Winter 1992. It is republished here by permission of the editors of *Hermathena*, with a few minor corrections, and some systematic changes requested by the publisher: the omission of diacritics on transliterated Greek words, ancient names in forms more familiar to non-specialist readers, and a more restricted use of capitals in poem and book titles. I should like to acknowledge the valuable help given to me, during the writing of this essay, by the late Marion Sarafis and by Dr George Koudoulis. All translations from Ristos' poems are my own.

Yannis Ritsos wrote his collection of seventeen poems *The fourth dimension* (*I tetarti diastasi*) between 1956 and 1972. The poems, averaging eighteen pages in length, are written in the dramatic monologue form and in twelve of them he uses classical myth. The easy manner in which he employs myth is due in part to that sense of a living relationship that Greeks generally have with their past, and in part to Ritsos' own completely unselfconscious attitude towards Ancient Greece. Its artefacts are part of the Greek landscape, untouched by any industrial revolution. This factor has strengthened a sense of historical continuity in Greece which is, moreover, reinforced by the continuity of the Greek language and by certain unchanging rituals and occupations of rural life. Ritsos can merge past and present so effortlessly that the anachronisms never offend the reader. There is a convincing sense of historical verisimilitude in his evocation of the ancient palaces of Mycenae and Thebes and in the camps at Troy. Simultaneously we feel a common humanity with those characters from the distant past who play their part in his extended allegory on contemporary life and human existence.

Ritsos, in using classical myths, objectivises the painful experiences of his childhood, the tensions which inevitably existed between himself and the Communist Party, and the terrible events of Greece's recent history, including the trauma of the military dictatorship which lasted from 1967 to 1974. The poems also convey his linear Marxist view of life, and his conviction that war is evil and futile. These themes all converge upon his overriding concern for the wholeness of the individual.

In "The dead house" (*To nekro spiti*) and "Under the shadow of the mountain" (*Kato ap' ton iskio tou vounou*), Ritsos makes a specific connection between the large house on the rock of Monemvasia where he spent his childhood and the fortress at ancient Mycenae. The women in these two poems, living in old houses that echo to the sounds of their own decay, see themselves as the surviving daughters of Agamemnon whose favourite pastime is hunting, a pastime which reflects that of Ritsos' father, Eleftherios Ritsos, with whom he had little affinity. In her book *The childhood and youth of my brother Yannis Ritsos,* his sister Loula Ritsou-Glezou describes how the men of the large Ritsos family made seasonal forays out from the rock of Monemvasia into their country estates to hunt down animals and bring the spoils back in triumph to the fortress, while the lonely womenfolk, confined to their quarters at the back of the house, against the mountain, had to sustain, with as much dignity as they could muster, the amorous exploits of their menfolk. The wife of Agamemnon, Clytemnestra, a prominent figure in these poems, is endowed with the qualities of Ritsos' beloved and long-suffering mother Eleftheria.

The association between the doomed Atreides and Ritsos' own family, decimated by illness and early death, is apparent in the imagery of blood in "The dead house". The elderly woman tells her visitor

> A red river flowed around our house;
> we turned away from the world outside
> later the world too forgot us.

Loula describes in her book the deaths of her mother and her elder brother Dimitris from tuberculosis, usually a fatal disease at that time, and how, in order to keep the one remaining daily servant with them, she had to bury the blood in the garden before dawn. "The dead house" and "Under the shadow of the mountain" echo as well with the trauma occasioned by the reversal of the Ritsos family fortunes. In "The dead house" the fall of the Atreides family is described:

> The last day the women slaves raised a cry and ran —
> a shrieking cry that stayed fixed in the shadowy corridor
> like a big fishbone in the throat of an unknown guest.
> . . . . . and they fled running
> their faces covered tight with their palms; but when they reached
> the top of the marble stair, behind the peristyle,
> they looked black, small, humpbacked,
> treacherous, malevolent, eager, deliberate, calculating,
> — they stopped for a moment, complete strangers to their earlier cry,
> they uncovered their faces,
> examined the stairs carefully so as not to fall
> although their feet had learned by heart the steps one by one
> and they knew the stair in its whole length.

Ritsos returns to this theme later in the poem, recalling more idyllic days in Monemvasia. The nostalgia for a lost paradise that echoes in the following passage is shared by many poets and writers of the generation of the thirties whose carefree adolescence was brought to an abrupt end by traumatic historical events.

> . . . . So the women slaves
> knew this stair well . . . . .
> at other times, on blithe days,
> when they carried their baking tins from the oven

or the big pitchers of wine from the basements
or the broad loaves and the butchered animals and the fruit
or armfuls of roses, carnations, and daisies
or modest olive branches and laurels bright from the morning dew —

on other days of weddings, baptisms, feasts, birthdays,
on days of triumph and glory when the dusty messenger
fell panting on this stair
and kissed the marble and wept
and announced his message in a manly, rather hoarse voice,
strange through the sound of his sobs.

Ritsos, having experienced the destruction of his land-owning class, understands these lonely elderly women who are haunted by the past and unable to involve themselves in the present, and who can only dwell on the terror of their imminent death. Loula Ritsou-Glezou remarks in her book that many of their female cousins, who would not marry outside their social class, died as impoverished and lonely spinsters. In this landscape of classical myth Mycenae's obdurate mountain sustains old worn-out social divisions to which the timid cling. Its oppressive presence nurtures a fear of life — is crushing to the spirit.

The woman in "Under the shadow of the mountain" says to her ancient nurse:

. . . yes, you would recognize me
by the style of my generation, by the look
that never bends, that never rests
on faces or things, but marches
straight on, alone, five metres above the helmets
of the extended firing squad.

In this poem Ritsos makes his social comments more obvious than he does in "The dead house". The narrator informs us in the epilogue that an elderly woman, the only survivor of the Atreides family, has died at last and her body has been found.

And some others gathered who had got out of a tourist bus. They wrapped her in a faded purple carpet and threw her into a makeshift grave. Shortly after that a torrent of rain fell. They squeezed hastily into the bus smelling with pleasure the broad aroma of soaked earth, stone and trees, as if the world were washing itself of some ancient miasma.

Ritsos himself was able to recover from the destruction of his class and to slough off the attitudes of that class, of the old social hierarchy which he came to regard as anachronistic; referring to people like these elderly women in his poems, he said in an interview published by the Communist newspaper *Rizospastis*, as part of a tribute to him on his eightieth birthday, "If you do not love people, if you are not a citizen, if you do not participate in the historical events of your country and of the world, it is as if you are a fugitive from life. You have nothing to live for. We can only pity these people, without excusing them."

The destructive tendency to dwell in the past is an unhappy feature of Greek life. Even the most recent literature reverberates with the trauma of the Civil War which took place between 1946 and 1949. The relentless cycle of murder and revenge in the Atreides family mirrors the savage fratricide of the Civil War, and the retributions which persisted for decades afterwards. The damage to the psyche is described in "The dead house" when the elderly woman recalls the battle-worn soldiers at Mycenae trying to hide their emotions as they sang their evocative village songs to the women and slaves in the kitchen:

> . . . the women
> listening to them wept hysterically
> tore their clothes, beseeched them
> and took them to their aprons like sick children
> whom they wanted to cure once and for all
> . . . to hold them
> close, deep down
> they alone to protect and keep them —
> and then to give birth to them
>
> at a more suitable moment, in a whiter house,
> in a more airy and sunny house with fewer shadows
> of columns, jars, murders, swords, glory, and coffins,
> with fewer secret holes in the walls . . . holes
> closed up by repairs, new plaster and whitewash,
> but always open further in, deep down, in memory.

The poem "Orestes" is a more specifically impassioned diatribe against the obdurate nursing of old grievances and hatreds. Orestes, accompanied by his faithful cousin Pylades arrives at the gate of Mycenae, a reluctant avenger, wearied already at the threshold of the act, scarcely able to endure the ranting voice of Electra shouting for revenge in the quiet moonlight, shouting, as Orestes says,

> ranting words, worn out, disinterred
> from linen chests "of the good old days" as our old people call them,
> like great flags unironed, into whose seams
> have penetrated naphthaline, denial, and silence — so old
> that they do not suspect their old age, and insist
> on rattling with archaic gestures above unsuspecting passers-by
> busy and tired.

He continues wearily:

> And she insists on preparing hydromel and food for the dead
> who no longer thirst and are not hungry — nor have they a mouth
> nor do they dream of reparation and revenge. She is always invoking
> their infallibility (what infallibility?) perhaps to escape
> from the responsibility for her own choice and decision.

Orestes recalls the wounded cow he and Pylades encountered on their way to Mycenae. Through the image of this gentle beast, whose blood dissolves in the flowing water she drinks, Ritsos seeks to reconcile the wronged to their grievances. He suggests that the wounded cow is a symbol of an harmonious order that humankind is forever desecrating with hatred and violence, and consequent damage to the human psyche.

Orestes fondly recalls his mother Clytemnestra with "her deep understanding, her tender tolerance / for everyone and all things". She was more in harmony with the world than was "that old little girl [...] / ascetic, repellent in her wisdom, / and unconnected". He expresses his sense of the unreal nature of this act of revenge extracted from him:

> . . . The years have passed.
> I don't feel any more — have I forgotten? Am I tired? I don't know.
> I am even touched by sympathy for the murderess — she has measured deep chasms,
> great knowledge made her eyes big in the darkness
> and she sees — she sees the inexhaustible, the unachievable and the unalterable.
> She sees me.

The image of Iphigeneia, the delicate, slaughtered girl in a white tunic, haunts Mycenae, Thebes and Troy. Her image is first conjured up by the slave cooks in the kitchen in "The dead house" as they stir into the cauldron with their wooden spoons the pottage of the terrible past which feeds the desire for further vengeance. Clytemnestra came to understand that justice, even for slaughtered *innocence*, is indeed unachievable by violence.

In the end Orestes carries out his perfunctory act of revenge, seeing it tentatively as a cleansing act. According to the myth he was pardoned by Athena and Apollo but here there is no *deus ex machina* to pass judgement on him. Orestes takes responsibility for his collusion in the act, and pardons himself. He says:

> I also want to see the murder of my father in the appeasing generality of death
> to forget him in the whole of death
> that awaits us all.

According to certain persons who knew Ritsos well, and whose testimony can be thoroughly relied upon, the poem "Orestes" also expresses Ritsos' exasperation with the intrusive, proprietary attitude that the Communist Party adopted towards him. He always refused however to sacrifice the integrity of his work, whether in relation to the Communist Party or to any right-wing dictatorship. There are certain remarks in "Orestes" which appear to corroborate the testimony of Ritsos' friends. The over burdened Orestes says to Pylades:

> How might it happen that we too could be independent with the beautiful
> joy of innocence, of religious tolerance, beyond everything,
> within everything, within ourselves —
> . . . without
> having to measure ourselves by the expectations and demands of others.

And again:

> . . . I don't want
> to be their theme, their clerk, their instrument, or their leader.
> I have my own life and have to lead it.

And yet again:

> . . . No one
> has the right to govern my eyes, my mouth, my hands,
> these feet of mine that walk on the earth.

It is significant that Ritsos was given his *Phylladio* — his membership booklet — by the Communist Party as late as July 1988, three years before his death.

In the poem "Philoctetes" (*Filoktitis*) Ritsos again deals with the problem of how the individual is to reconcile his personal convictions with the claims of society. The monologue is spoken by Neoptolemus whose task it was to persuade Philoctetes to leave the island on which he was abandoned by the Greeks on their way to Troy, and help defeat the Trojans with his invincible weapons.

In referring to this recent and unwilling recruit to the Trojan War also as *Neos*, the Young Man, Ritsos makes him a spokesman for all time against the evil of war. Neoptolemus describes to Philoctetes how, during the protracted war with Troy, the selfishness, the greed for booty, the competition for primacy among the leaders, the cynicism are far removed from the noble behaviour associated with legendary heroes. The atmosphere at Troy is permeated by dread:

> . . . We heard the big thud, when a tree
> fell to the ground, and silence hid in fear
> behind our shoulders. It was as if I already saw
> the Wooden Horse . . . I was preparing myself
> for the huge, futile leap into the unknown.

Neoptolemus postulates that, since Philoctetes had foreseen the reality of war, the snake-bite at the altar had effectively released him from its horrors and the brutalizing effect on the psyche. He describes the soldiers asleep, "snoring, reviling a dream cow". Despite the damage done to their natures they are dimly conscious still that their natural instincts are towards harmony, not conflict. In the tribute to Yannis Ritsos in *Rizospastis* in 1990 he is quoted as saying: "Our inclination is towards well-being, happiness and peace."

Neoptolemus also points out that while Philoctetes' wound is visible, *his* wound is no less real for being invisible. Evoking the oppressive atmosphere in the house of his father Achilles, that heroic prototype whose overpowering personality reflects that of Ritsos' own father, he says

> . . . father's shadow would darken the whole house,
> closing doors and windows from top to bottom
> . . .
> They prepared the food for the dead along with our food . . . in secret foundries
> day and night they hammered shields and javelins . . . in underground workshops
> they sculpted busts and statues of the gods of war and men of war (but not
> of athletes and poets) as well as hundreds of funeral slabs
> with beautiful, naked youths, always standing,
> disguising with their vertical stance
> the eternal horizontal attitude of death.

Neoptolemus eloquently convinces Philoctetes that his presence, even more than the surrendering to them of his weapons, is vital to the Greeks, not only to help end the senseless slaughter, but through his suffering and his wisdom to help heal the wounds in the aftermath of war. Philoctetes does not need to put on the mask of action given to him by Neoptolemus to hide his "transparent distant face". In the epilogue Ritsos says, "That mask remained up above in the rocks outside the cave, shining in the mysterious serenity of the night, with a strange incomprehensible affirmation." As a pacifist, Philoctetes is nevertheless persuaded that he must fight with his fellow countrymen to bring an end to the evil of the Trojan War. *Rizospatis* in the review already mentioned, quoted Ritsos' remarks expressing his pride in the resistance of his fellow countrymen to fascism during the Second World War. Ritsos himself was active in the Cultural Section of the National Liberation Front which he joined in 1942.

War is also the theme of the poem "Helen" (*Eleni*), which was written in 1970 and published in 1972 when the Junta had embarked on a cautious "liberalization" programme. Ritsos, in this poem, clearly took advantage of the relaxation of censorship. Right-wing dictatorships in Greece had always tended to see a direct link between Modern and Ancient Greece, ignoring the cultural heritage of four hundred years of Turkish rule. The classical myths therefore always seem to be a prominent feature of their education and propaganda programme. This is probably why Ritsos so *harshly* debunks, at this time, the myth that war is heroic and glorious.

In her repulsive physical decay Helen has become the symbol of the ugliness of war and, seeing her as such, visitors who persist in hankering after the chimera of national glory and in wanting to see a still beautiful woman, flee from her, leaving her at the mercy of her cruelly impudent slaves, who are waiting for her to die. She assures her middle-aged admirer that the Trojan War with its horrors was pointless. She no longer believes in anything; words exist simply to fill up the emptiness of concepts.

At the end of her monologue Helen conveys the histrionic aspect of myth-making. She recalls the scene on the walls of Troy when she felt herself to be lifted up into heaven as an immortal with the ecstatic soldiers on both sides worshipping her, and compares their transports to those of an audience in a shabby theatre. The implication here is that both the audience in the shabby theatre and the soldiers in the chaotic bloodstained theatre of war had been temporarily carried away into a willing suspension of disbelief. Helen sees war as a theatre for the display of monstrous egotism by the few, while the countless dead, the extras in the drama, remain anonymous.

In describing the dull aftermath of war, with the inevitable nostalgia for glory, Helen is clearly also referring to the stultifying atmosphere imposed by the Junta that any visitor to Greece at that time will recognize:

>   . . . the newspapers with the same
> format, length and names
>   . . . I no longer read them.
>   Every so often
> flags on the balconies, national ceremonies, military parades,

like clockwork.

With wicked humour Ritsos has Helen speak of the conjugal boredom suffered by herself and her resentful husband Menelaus in Argos under this dispensation:

> I no longer went to the ceremonies. My husband would come back sweating
> and tuck into his food, smacking his lips, at the same time chewing
> over past glories and stale resentments . . .

Then she would daydream about Odysseus, back in Ithaca, who was refusing to answer letters, even urgent telegrams,

> delaying his return, the cunning man — on the pretext
> of exaggerated dangers . . .
> . . . The Moving Rocks
> have gone elsewhere, to a place further in — I feel them
> motionless, softened — more frightening than before — they do not crush,
> they drown in a thick, black fluid . . . no one escapes

Helen's description of the irrational and incomprehensible gestures of the dead who haunt the house connect this poem to the collection of short poems *Scripture of the blind* (*Grafi tiflou*) published in 1979, in which the deliberately evasive gestures of the protagonists are symbolic of the repression and fear imposed by the military dictatorship. Helen comments: "Our own strange and unfamiliar gestures have a calm, inexplicable beauty and a deep pain, have they not?" Ritsos refers to our gestures of self-defence against the damage being inflicted on us by whatever dispensation we ourselves have helped to create.

In "The return of Iphigeneia" (*I epistrofi tis Ifiyenias*), Ritsos also emphasizes the theatrical element in the making of myths, especially for hollow causes. Iphigeneia and Orestes have returned to Mycenae which is now "all nettles and thorns and the keys thrown away", and the Sunday strollers in the square indifferent to "the statue of a living girl whom they killed young". However, she blushes to remember her heroic speech at the altar at Aulis:

> in my shame there was also a secret pleasure
> like a successful actor would feel, perhaps.

Ritsos uses the alternative version of the myth in which she was replaced at the last moment by a hind and taken by Artemis to be her priestess at Tauris. To this end her mother Clytemnestra had made for her, when she was a child, a hind's mask which she always wore for the festival at Lent. Iphigeneia recalls "the general deep complicity:

> . . . I just felt
> they had stuck on my shoulders
> huge cardboard wings that every so often came unstuck with their weight, taking
> a piece of my skin — and they would stick them
> onto my wounds again . . . Soon
> adjustment was achieved without great effort.

In *Scripture of the blind*, Ritsos develops the theme that we can so easily and dangerously assume the persona of the invisible masks we put on.

Another victim of the Trojan War is Ajax, a simple and loveable man, driven mad by the unjust behaviour of his fellow fighters who exploited his physical strength, cheating him of his rightful place in the annals of the war. The poem "Ajax" opens with him prostrate among the animals he has slaughtered in a paranoic frenzy, believing them to be the hated Agamemnon, Odysseus and other Greek warriors mocking him, disguised as animals. The tension in this poem is focussed on Ajax's struggle to emerge from his mental chaos, to achieve balance. In recalling the fleeting moments during the war, when an alternative state of being was glimpsed, he remembers how the soldiers, washing at the water's edge, were prompted by the rosy light of dawn to look down at their reflections and to note briefly, once more, their physical beauty, before the spectre of the sun appeared out of the sea calling them to battles and vainglory. He realizes at last that he has been thoroughly deceived by the lure of trophies:

> My old feats seem like lies to me now.
> . . .
> I spent all my strength fighting phantoms
> . . .
> Failure and mockery are nothing. The vanish with us.
> I never asked for slaves, admirers, luxuries. I want no more than a man
> to speak with as an equal to an equal — where is he? Only our death
> is our equal . . . (pp. 94, 96, 97 in the present volume)

The feeling of bitter isolation, in this deeply sad monologue to his silent wife, echoes with the post-war betrayal of leftist hopes, and with alienation within the family and among former comrades that is a recurring theme in the modern Greek novel. Helen too says:

> A, yes . . . how many
> sacrifices and defeats upon defeats and yet more battles, for things already decided
> by others while we were absent.

Another alienated figure is Agamemnon who returns to Mycenae battle-weary and disillusioned. His arrival is announced in "The dead house" by the sobbing messenger kneeling on the stair:

> he announced the brilliant victory
> with two thousand dead — not counting the wounded —
> finally he announced the arrival of our general
> with many banners and flags and carriages and slaves
> and a wound in the middle of his forehead — he said —
> like a new, superb eye, from which death stared,
> and the general could now see into the depths
> of landscapes, things, people
> as if it were all transparent glass . . .
> They all listened (myself included) as if petrified,
> all anxious and bowed and tearless . . .

Agamemmnon clearly sees, apart from the hollowness of victory and the futility of the Trojan War, that the sacrifices and the suffering have been due to the general collusion in that war, that the guilt must be shared by all. "This vision," he says, "neither enemy nor friend can forgive." In a mood of deep sadness and tired tenderness he speaks to Clytemnestra (he doesn't know if she is listening to him) expressing his tragic sense of their wasted lives:

> How did we let the hours slip by, trying stupidly
> and so hard to procure a place in the perception of others. Never a second
> to ourselves in so many long summers, to see
> the shadow of a bird on the corn — a small trireme
> on a golden sea — we might have sailed in it
> for silent trophies, more glorious conquests. But we didn't.

They didn't make that voyage of the heart.

The only person in this cast of characters who made that journey is Chrysothemis, the daughter of Agamemnon who had always tended to be overlooked. This elderly, obscure woman, to her surprise, finds herself being interviewed at Mycenae by a young woman journalist.

Chrysothemis, whose name "golden order" implies a sense of harmony with the world, has retained her childlike, fervent response to beauty. This enchanting woman, in recalling certain moments in her life, has much of the charm of the poet himself. His sister Loula describes in her book how, when she and Yannis were in school at Yithion, a bat flew into the schoolroom where the girls stayed during break-times. Yannis went into this forbidden territory to rescue the bat from the shrieking, panic-stricken girls. Chyrsothemis describes a similar incident at Mycenae while her parents and Iphigeneia were quarelling loudly:

> . . . their mouths got bigger full of darkness
> . . .
> At that moment a bat came in the window
> carrying a few stars, a piece of velvet night,
> two leaves of mulberry tree, the soft bleat
> of a small sheep beside the river, at the hour when the shepherd's star
> trembles in the water . . .
> . . . Suddenly the grown-ups were silent.
>
> Perhaps they harkened to that bleat. They may have been afraid
> of the distant, the beautiful, the unknown. However they heard it. Then mother
> grabbed a napkin from the table and chased the bat;
> the oil lamps nearly went out. I loved her very much
> my mother, in this posture — even though she was once more
> arrogant, aggressive, commanding — with the white napkin fluttering
> in one hand — like a one-winged bird that cannot fly. In her big eyes
> sparkled secretly the desire to go away into the night, into the whole of the night.
> Then *I* took a napkin and put it like a second wing in her other hand.
> She smiled with complicity; and then said, very angry: "Have you gone mad?"

> . . . The quarrel
> began again louder. It didn't bother me. I was quiet. I just pitied them.
> I too had my secret allies —

While the other characters in the poems have glimpsed from time to time a possible harmony between themselves and the world, the saintly Chrysothemis was *born* into this fourth dimension. She recalls how, as a child, she used to regard with uncomprehending amazement the histrionics of the grown-ups:

> . . . They would raise their arms
> high in the air as if they were holding up a beam
> that was just about to fall.
> . . . They would open their mouths
> rapaciously, rhetorically, mournfully — a hole filled with darkness
> and deep within shone dim an ancient iron rickety stairway.

Ritsos, through the wisdom of Chrysothemis, urges a reconciliation to the terrible past. She says:

> . . . I learned very early
> that no one can avert anything.
> . . .
> we never learned what was to blame, who was to blame.

Turning towards the garden she points out to the young journalist

> the little statue of the daughter who was slaughtered small as a tooth
> that troubled you a lot and you had it taken out, and it doesn't pain you any more.

Chrysothemis acknowledges that she was blessed in having an infinite capacity to respond to beauty:

> Each day leaves us something for the night — it is difficult to sleep sometimes
> if you haven't something beautiful to confront the dark that lies in ambush.

In the epilogue we are told that the interview was printed as a book which ran into several editions:

> And on spring and summer evenings you will very often see young couples, old ladies, or even footballers, leaving a small bunch of violets or a few wild flowers on her tomb, beside the large official wreaths that are placed there by various artistic, philanthropic or political organizations.

While we cannot all be saints and poets, most of us can identify with Ismene, the sister of Antigone. Chrysothemis saw herself as being on the edge of events and was allowed to stay there. Ismene, on the other hand, found herself unwillingly placed in the middle of the struggle between Antigone and her uncle Creon. The sons of Oedipus, in a battle for the throne, had killed each other. Creon buried Eteocles but left Polynices unburied, since he had fought against Thebes with the help of the Argives. Against Creon's edict Antigone buried the body of Polynices, an act in which Ismene refused to take part. Creon is symbolically portrayed. When they are preparing the bodies of Antigone and her intended bridegroom Haemon for burial,

> Outside at the peristyle, you could hear the wild groaning of Creon
> the clanging of his sword emphasizing the silence of his guards.

Ismene comments that Antigone and Polynices on the contrary

> had a very personal perception of justice. They couldn't see
> the justice of others or general injustice.

However, Ismene, in her monologue to the son of one of their tenant farmers is more concerned with Antigone's motives for sacrificing herself. She suggests that fear of life impelled her sister towards an early death:

> . . . Those who are always afraid
> (as for example my sister) have not the strength to bend.
> My sister regulated everything by a must or must not,
> as if she were the harbinger of that future religion
> which divided the world into two (the here and the herafter) which divided
> the human body into two, rejecting that part from the waist downwards.
> . . .
> . . . Never
> would she let Haemon touch her hand
> . . .
> You would think my sister was ashamed to be a woman. Perhaps
> this was her happiness. Perhaps because of this she died.

For Antigone, denial of life becomes an unassailable virtue. Ismene describes her

> . . . carrying around
> her black arrogance at our parties.
> . . . And if, sometimes,
> she went to help at table, to bring a plate, a pitcher,
> you would think she was carrying a naked skull in her palms
> and placing it among the amphora. No one could be drunk after that.

Her sacrifice was not the selfless act that it seemed. In Ismene's eyes she had transformed her fear of life into egoistic heroism.

Ismene, preparing Antigone's body for burial, dresses her in rich attire and paints her face so that she looks very like Ismene herself. She says, "In her death she had become a woman at last." On the other hand the ageing Ismene confesses in her monologue to the feeling of existing in a vacuum that also afflicts the women in "The dead house" and "Under the shadow of the mountain". In the epilogue she views her physical decay in the mirror and decides not to admit her former visitor, the young man, with whom she had an assignation. Instead she paints her face again into "a plaster mask, the eyes huge, very black". It is significant that she puts on Antigone's ill-fitting brown dress, before swallowing what looks like aspirin, and lying down calmly and smilingly to await death. In putting on Antigone's dress Ismene is identifying with her sister in her desire for death, but it is as if the cynical Ismene also tacitly acknowledges at last a dimension in herself that was tragically lacking. Ritsos is perhaps suggesting here that a combination of Antigone, with her courage and commitment, and Ismene, with her perceptive qualities, her common sense and good humour, would have produced a balanced person, a whole person.

In the poem "Phaedra", the young Hippolytus, impervious to Phaedra's love for him, displays an imbalance similar to that of Antigone: "The holiness of the will. The victory of denial" are words of Hippolytus that Phaedra scoffs at in her impassioned monologue to him. "What victory?" she says.

> . . . Holiness before sin
> I don't believe it — impossible, cowardly, I say —
> and tributes to the gods: ploys to avoid suffering.

She scoffs also at his image of himself as a chaste hunter:

> How did the hunt go today? I've never understood
> what you hunt. You never bring back your trophies.
> as the others do —
> . . . I believe
> that you never kill deer — the favourite animal of your Goddess. Everyone
> talks of your accurate aim. I haven't seen anything of it.

Hippolytus' affinity with Antigone is obvious. The cross given to him by Artemis is a crucifix.

Phaedra's beautiful speech to him burns with the intensity of her unabating passion for him. Although Ritsos clearly focuses his sympathy on Phaedra, her obsessive love nevertheless impels her to a spiteful act of revenge. In Ritsos' poem it is she who dies first. She hangs herself, leaving a note for her husband Theseus, accusing her step-son of attempting to rape her. The shadows of statues in the garden of Aphrodite and Artemis fall crosswise on the body of the hanged woman.

Ritsos suggests, however, that some alleviation would be possible even in this extreme case of the dualism of body and soul. During the monologue it is clear that Hippolytus was drawn to Phaedra; she recalls how he once put his head on her shoulder for a fleeting moment, meeting her on the stairway of her house in Athens. They could have met on middle ground if his narcissistic denial of his physical nature had permitted him to show even a little generosity of spirit. Phaedra, in her bitter remarks, exposes this lack in him:

> What *do* you hunt by the way? Perhaps
> you offer all your game to Artemis? All the same I would love
> a deep blue feather for my hat — you could dedicate
> something to me too perhaps.

It is significant that Hippolytus *kneels* while listening to the sentence pronounced upon him by Theseus. He sees not only his own part in the tragedy, but also the harm done to himself by his stubborn insistence on wearing the mask of holiness that so tormented Phaedra.

Phaedra on the contrary declares:

> . . . I have confessed. Holiness
> humility lying I don't hold with. I have torn off
> the mask and thrown it at your feet.

Iphigenia also recalls how her mother Clytemnestra never avoided anything, never retreated; she wore jewellery only to divert attention from her too great capacity to love. Philoctetes the pacifist refused to wear the mask of action when in his heart he knew that he had to help end the Trojan War.

The motif of the mask is most prominent in the poem "Ismene" (*Ismini*), when Ismene recalls the masks of self-defence worn against the all too frequently imposed trauma of change and uncertainty:

> Wars, revolutions, counter-revolutions (how many times did the same things happen) —
> a pile of ashes in the squares from the fires they lit
> for big feasts and for the dead — the same ashes;
> . . . Intrigues, briberies, betrayals;
> Thebans, Argives, Corinthians, Spartans, Athenians. Who was really governing?
> a secret power moving the strings from a distance.

The trauma of change that Ismene continues to describe relates also to the contemporary situation in Greece in 1971:

> Men wearing masks came out at midnight with bright flashlights
> people in fear mixing together again. One afternoon
> high up in a student's garret a flute could be heard.
> . . .
> a covered lorry passed; everyone scattered; the flute was silent.
> . . .
> The sun came out again; nothing was changed
> . . . The same people with different masks
> . . . they would make gestures, open their mouths wide.
> Not a sound, not a cry issued — a black hole in the air;
> they could have been shouting "long live" or "down with" — I couldn't make anything out
> only fear stood out.

The danger is that, as Iphigeneia says when describing the hind's mask placed upon her, "Soon adjustment was achieved without great effort." This truth is demonstrated when Chyrsothemis, in the typically irrational imagery that Ritsos uses for this purpose, remembers the day after the fall of the Atreides:

> The next day I stood facing the deserted square
> whitewashed with silence. Five eggs lay
> at the base of an old lamp-post. A woman came out of the stable
> very cautiously. She took the eggs, which immediately

turned red. Another woman, watching from the window opposite said:
"Have your hens started laying red eggs?" And the first one said:
"The dawn has made them red," and she hid them in the pockets of her apron.

The feeling of existence in a void afflicts especially the elderly women who have opted out of the world. They live in grand, ancient houses that are in a state of collapse. "Yet it isn't collapse," as Ismene says. The concrete objects that litter these poems, the detritus from the past, have nowhere to fall. There is no foundation; there is no ceiling. In a radio broadcast in Prague in 1962 Ritsos talked about the feelings of uncertainty, vagueness, and incomprehensibility that permeate modern life.

The longing for surcease from the trauma of existence, which the characters in theses poems express in various degrees, reaches its apotheosis in "Persephone" (*Persefoni*). In a reversal of the myth it is *she* who first falls deeply in love with Hades during a visit he makes from the Underworld to her mother Demeter. Hades eventually sends his old clothes to Demeter to be given to the poor. As a consequence the young girl is even more erotically inclined towards him, so that she is far from being an unwilling victim when he abducts here:

> . . . I wasn't at all afraid
> . . .
> And then I felt his rough muscular arm
> wrapped round my waist to subdue my resistance — what resitance? —
> I was not myself.
> . . . "Are you aftaid?" he said to me.
> (How weak the very strong are — they are always afraid
> we don't fear them as we should — beautiful, unsuspecting
> in their childish ignorance.) "Yes, " I said — "I am afraid,"
> and he held me more tightly to him.

On her return to the earth she lies in a darkened room peevishly complaining about the blinding light, and pining for the grey, static existence with Hades. She relates to her young companion how the terrible dog Cerberus, with whom she developed a not unloving relationship, watched her every move, her slightest gesture. This scenario reflects Ritsos' own experience while he was under house arrest in Samos from 1968 to 1970 and thereafter until 1974 under constant surveillance at his flat in Athens. The claustrophobia that Persephone relives becomes so intolerable that she suddenly leaps up from her bed, and, flinging open the windows, faces the blazing afternoon sun. In the epilogue, "She stands there in the blinding light like a statue that gradually comes to life."

Ritsos never doubted the capacity of the human being for spiritual regeneration, a belief that held fast, despite the terrible experiences that people of his generation lived through. As a man who was deeply committed to socialist principles, he held to his conviction that we can break free from the cycle of turbulent changes — but in order to do so we have to begin with ourselves. The woman in "Under the shadow of the mountain" says: "We destroy ourselves more than events or time destroy us." During the interview in the newspaper *Rizospastis* in 1990 Ritsos said: "In doing some act, making a gesture, giving a look of compassion, we are turning to our fellow human beings. In this way we will find hope again. We will find our faith again."

The motif of light in these poems reflects our instinct towards wholeness, towards harmony with the world, towards the fourth dimension. Neoptolemus recalls a cool, quiet room at his home, with a line of Kouroi against one wall, statues offered to Apollo the god of harmony, the god of light. Iphigeneia leaves Mycenae to attend her shrine at Vravona — bringing with her the empty cage in which her mother Clytemnestra had kept three successive parrots to whom she taught to say one word — "Light".

Orestes leaves Mycenae after carrying out his act of revenge: "Then in the middle of the Gate of the Lions stood a large cow, gazing right into the morning sky, her huge black motionless eyes, staring." The wounded cow reminds us of the cattle sacred to the sun that were slaughtered by Odysseus' men who suffered the consequences of their careless act. Ritsos said that he always looked back to Homer.

RITSOS IN BELFAST

MARJORIE CHAMBERS

This essay was first published in a Greek translation in *Themata Logothechnias* (*Literary Topics*) vol. 5, 1997. The original English version is published here for the first time. Page references following quotations refer to the translations of the poems in the present volume. I am indebted to Marian Sarafis for introducing me to Olympia Papadouka, who gave me valuable information and put me in touch with Zizi Makri, and to Dr Louis Muinzer, who gave generously of his time to produce the reading and arrange the venue — all four of them sadly no longer with us. My thanks also to my son, Michael Chambers, who synchronized Beethoven's music with the reading of *The Moonlight Sonata*.

Shortly after Yannis Ritsos' death in 1990, the Delphic Players, under the direction of Dr Louis Muinzer, presented a rehearsed reading at the Lyric Theatre, Belfast, of my translations of three dramatic poems by Ritsos: *The Moonlight Sonata, The prison tree and the women* and *Farewell*. Ritsos' oeuvre being so extensive, the last two poems in the trilogy came into my hands almost by chance. Placing them beside *The Moonlight Sonata*, one of Ritsos' best known poems, the theme of imprisonment that I discerned in them, in one form or another, seemed to me to convey a sympathetic echo of our experience during the troubled decades of the 1970s and 1980s in Northern Ireland.

In *The Moonlight Sonata* (pp. 57–64), for example, first published in 1956 and later included in a volume of existentialist poems entitled *The fourth dimension*, the dancing bear appears as a symbol of Greece, worn out by the terrible events of her recent past and having neither the strength nor the will to emerge from the neo-colonial condition in which she found herself. This dilemma reminds us of the protracted reluctance of some sections of our community to find a way out from a situation which is not acceptable to a large minority of our people.

> The tired bear walks on in the knowledge of her loneliness, not knowing where
>   or why —
> she is heavy now, and can no longer dance on her hind legs or wear her lace cap
>   to amuse the children, the idlers, the exacting,
> and all she wants to do is to lie on the ground
> letting them step on her belly, so playing her last game,
> showing her fearsome strength in resignation
> . . .
> But who can play that game to the end? (p. 61)

The elderly woman in the poem is also a prisoner, entrapped in her past, despite her belated efforts to come to terms with the changes that time has brought about. She identifies with the bear in her lack of will to free herself from the impasse in which she suffers. At the end of the poem it is doubtful whether she will ever leave the decaying house that is haunted by the ghosts of her past.

> Often I run across to the chemist for an aspirin,
> at other times I cannot stir myself and I am left with my headache
> to hear inside the walls the hollow sound of the water-pipes
> or I brew a coffee, and always absent-minded,
> I forget and prepare two — who is to drink the other? —
> silly really, I leave it on the window-sill to get cold
> or sometimes I also drink the second, gazing out the window at the chemist's green globe
> like the green light of a silent train coming to take me
> . . .
> Ah, you are leaving? Goodnight. No, I won't come. Goodnight.
> I'll go out in a little while. Thank you. Because I must
> get out of this crumbling house at last.
> I should see something of the town   . . .   (p. 63)

The actress Brenda Shaw, who read this dramatic monologue with such sensitivity, conveyed all its nuances of nostalgia, sadness, fear, and despair — which surely echoed for the audience the dismay and sustained anxiety following change and uncertainty, the despair of ever finding a way out of entrenched beliefs, the recurring temptation to turn in on oneself, the longing to escape from a seemingly intractable situation, the very real possibility of injury and death which have been prevalent in our society for a quarter of a century. This state of mind was aptly captured in a painting of the 70s by the artist Catherine McWilliams sombrely depicting a typical Belfast scene of the time, overlaid with rainbow colours, and with the caption: "I want to be anywhere but here."

The feeling of claustrophobic despair that was familiar to us is emphasised in the poem through the significantly recurring metaphor of the circle. The old bear dances on the lead for the crowd gathered round her, indifferent to "the rings on her lips" (p. 61). For the woman, the image of the circle invokes terror, a threatening paralysis of the will. The rim of the glass she raises to her lips is "a round razor" (p. 60). She sees "a hole of silence" when she lifts the cup from the table (p. 62). In a surrealistic scene she feels as if she were floating around her kitchen where familiar objects assume monstrous shapes, or evade her touch. In her spells of giddiness, the seductive moon, "a hole in the world's skull" (p. 62), threatens to draw her down in a vortex of complete surrender to defeat.

The silent pause from the audience, after the last notes of Beethoven's accompanying music had died away, was an indication of how much the listeners were moved by the confession of this lonely woman, with her very human weaknesses.

During the interval following the reading of this poem, we enjoyed the generous hospitality of the then administrator of the Lyric Theatre, Mike Blair. Among the forty or so people present were students of mine who had read *The Moonlight Sonata* with me in Greek, and who had contributed some of the comments on the poem that I have just made.

The second part of the event began with *The prison tree and the women* (pp. 79–85). This verse drama was written in Prague in 1962, and was performed there as a theatre piece in 1965. It was inspired by an exhibition of woodcuts by the engraver Zizi Makri, who for many years had been a friend of the poet. She herself was imprisoned "for political reasons" in the Averof prison in Athens, 1962–63.

A documentary book on this prison, during the period 1947–50, was compiled by the actress Olympia Papadouka, who was herself a prisoner in Averof, and who, with Yannis Ritsos, was a member of the Athens People's Theatre, founded by EAM (the National Liberation Front) at Trikkala in 1945. The Averof prison was built in 1890 for two hundred inmates. In 1947–50 twelve hundred prisoners were confined there.

Within these prison walls the women, from all walks of life, used their various skills to help one another maintain dignity and sanity in conditions which were always degrading. Activities of prison life were described touchingly and often humorously through song and dance. Olympia Papadouka writes: "we found ourselves in prison, but we were free in our souls and in our ideals."

In her book is a photograph of the prison yard, with a huge palm tree in the middle. During a phone call to Budapest, Zizi Makri also told me that this tree (which features in her woodcuts) was "the only living thin in Averof, and therefore meant so much to the women prisoners. They used to stroll around it, and often danced around it to lift their spirit."

In Ritsos' poem, the tree is the focal point, a symbol of the undefeated human spirit:

FIFTH WOMAN:
>many times, during sleep, lying down, we remain standing in the posture of the tree
>— perhaps this tree must not let us rest,

FIRST WOMAN:
>must not let us forget,

FOURTH WOMAN:
>must not let us die.

FIFTH WOMAN:
>This tree keeps watch without effort or display.

FIRST WOMAN:
>Its most delicate branches spread in our fingers;

FIFTH WOMAN:
>when we eat, a yellow leaf happens to fall next to the bread from Mary's hands —
>none of us is surprised — and sometimes a small green twig happens to move. (p. 81)

The mood of calm optimism and faith in human kind is not easily achieved, however, against the prevailing fear expressed by the women:

SECOND WOMAN:
>and green leaves peep out of Mary's hair — so much that we are afraid they will be seen, the keys will sound in the guard's belt, a glass will fall from above and break on the paving stones,

ALL TOGETHER:
>the words we concealed will be heard — perhaps for this reason sparrows are so clumsy sometimes when they hop on the ground. (p. 85)

These lines evoke an immediate sympathy, bringing to mind the wariness we all felt about saying the wrong word at the wrong time, our particular dilemma in a divided society, expressed by Seamus Heaney in his poem "Whatever you say, say nothing".

Yet the mood of *The prison tree and the women* is ultimately uplifting: "and green leaves peep out of Mary's hair" (p. 85) recalls the regenerative powers associated with the image of the Byzantine Virgin. And the tree is constant. Its shadow becomes a ladder towards the sun, which is a recurring symbol of the ascending course of life in the poetry of Ritsos. The lasting freedom that the women struggle towards is expressed in the image of the stars:

> The women lay down. Outside the walls and in the room there were many stars, indescribably many stars, like notched wheels, like pentagrams, like carriages, like calm animals, like birds, like broad leaves — and they shone so much that Helen was unable to sleep. (p. 85)

The audience had no difficulty in empathizing with the imprisoned women. During the decade of the 70s particularly, physical freedom in Northern Ireland was also curtailed. One felt like a prisoner in one's own home, which moreover was not necessarily a safe haven for all of us. Venturing out from our homes, we were confronted with barriers, body searches, security checks, and soldiers in the streets.

The audience responded warmly to this poem, which gently radiates faith in human kind. The modest heroism of the women, so truthfully portrayed, recalls those few well known, and many not so well known, women who continue to work with quiet determination for peace in our community.

In view of our history, we in Ireland can also appreciate something of what it must be like to live in the tragically divided Cyprus. The third poem, *Farewell* (pp. 65–78), was prompted by an incident that took place there in 1957, during the struggle for *Enosis* ("Union" with Greece). Grigoris Afxendiou, the young deputy leader of EOKA (the National Organization of the Cypriot Combatants), had taken refuge in a cave at Machairas Monastery. The cave was eventually discovered and he and his fellow fighters were ordered to give themselves up; Afxendiou refused, and perished in the cave.

Ritsos, again using the dramatic monologue form, imagines in *Farewell* the thoughts of such a man trapped in the burning cave, face to face with death. On the face of it this poem would be expected to appeal particularly to terrorists and their sympathizers. It would therefore perhaps be timely to mention at this point that the readers and the audience included both Catholics and Protestants. The poem was read by an Englishman, Dr Matt Dring, a lecturer in the Faculty of Science at Queen's University Belfast, who gave a moving and sensitive reading. The fact that Dr Dring was more than willing to read the poem is a measure of its spiritual quality, transcending national identities. It is a loving and convincing portrayal of the purity of intention of Afxendiou, who is presented as a romantic revolutionary. In Ritsos' mind, Afxendiou becomes a Christ-like figure, a saint purified by fire, a symbol of the indomitable spirit of the Greek nation.

The love Afxendiou expresses for his country is akin to the love for our own country that unites all sections of our community:

> It was spring then. We were sitting down at the port in Famagusta,
> and I know now — I didn't know then — life was beautiful (and is
> perhaps always more beautiful — becomes more beautiful — as we make it so)
> the ears of corn, the citrons, the orchards, the houses, the women, the boats were beautiful —
> it was beautiful when the water's reflections played on the sides of ships — beautiful too
> the shadows of ships in the water. (p. 70)

The reading reached a fitting climax with this poem, where the sun of faith shines with a dazzling light. The mood of sustained fervour culminates in an elated confirmation of faith in human kind, reaffirmed though the sacrifice of Afxendiou. The value of this poem lies in the fact that it rises far above the merely partisan:

> If I regret anything it is that I shall no longer be able to do things for you
> (not with fame, or concept, or legend, but with these hands of mine).
> Let's say I too could shoot a rifle in the air on the feast of liberation
> or load onto a large truck a hundred sacks of bread, two hundred of potatoes,
> or carry that old woman's load of sticks in the wood
> or lift up the old mule driver's horse that has fallen in the mud one rainy morning
> or kick the ball the children of my country are playing with in the field one afternoon
> or give my friend a cuff one evening for telling a silly joke
> or share out, on a day work went well, a paper bag of sweets among the small children in our
>   neighbourhood   .   .   . (p. 74)

And in his parting remarks, Afxendiou says

> So now, with deep certainty I can say to you
> as I drive my car once more straight and neat on an asphalt road in Cyprus
> on a calm blue morning — I can say: "Our virtue
> is in our usefulness to one another." All right, my brothers. Here
> brotherhood for us and for all men is not impossible.
> Here differences will vanish in a smile   .   .   . (p. 76)

The poetry reading ended with this eloquent plea for peace and reconciliation. As the audience was lingering afterwards in the foyer — where the reading took place — a lady approached me (I don't know if she was Catholic or Protestant) to say how beautiful she found the language of *Farewell*, and asked me if she could use some of the material to read with the handicapped children whom she taught.

So, for an afternoon at the Lyric Theatre, Yannis Ritsos had inspired and enchanted us with the humanity and beauty of his poetry, and he had reminded us again that, as Charles Dickens emphasized in *Bleak House*, and indeed throughout his work, we are all closer together than we think.

RITSOS IN DUBLIN

MARJORIE CHAMBERS

This is the text (published here for the first time) of a short talk delivered at Trinity College Dublin on 25 March 2017 at a meeting of the Greek Community of Ireland, as an introduction to a performance of *The Moonlight Sonata* in Greek by two actors who had come from Athens, Marios Iordanou and Sophia Kazantzian. Their performance followed a rehearsed reading of my English translation of the poem (pages 57–64 in the present volume) by Paul Corcoran, Ellen Finn and Andrew Beazley, students in the Department of Classics of Trinity College Dublin, under the direction of Patrick Sammon. Much earlier, in 1991, the translation had been presented as a rehearsed reading at The Lyric Theatre, Belfast (see pp. 217–18 above.).

When Yannis Ritsos died in 1990, his international reputation was well established. He came from a wealthy, landowning family in Monemvasia. When he was a child, his father lost his fortune, partly through gambling, and partly as a consequence of the war with Turkey (1919–22). Ritsos' mother and elder brother died of tuberculosis, and he himself spent some years of his youth in sanatoria.

During the Second World War and the Civil War, he became involved in the leftist cause, and was imprisoned in various camps between 1948 and 1952, and later, under the Colonels' Regime between 1967 and 1974.

During the last decades of his life, he became active in the cause of peace. In 1979, he was awarded the International Peace Prize from the World Peace Organisation. In 1986, he was a founder member, with Mikis Theodorakis, of the Greek–Turkish Friendship Society.

When I was teaching Modern Greek at Queen's University, one of my students brought me from Greece a recording, dated 1958, of Yannis Ritsos reading *I Sonata tou Selinofotos* (*The Moonlight Sonata*). On the back of the record sleeve was a photograph of Ritsos, without his distinguished-looking beard. He was caught in a moment of laughing. I was immediately impressed; how could a person who had been through the German Occupation, the Civil war in Greece, as well as poverty, sanatoria, and prison camps — how could he laugh like that, without a hint of irony or cynicism? During the previous twenty years, there hadn't been much laughter like this in Northern Ireland. In the early 1980s, when I looked at the photograph, I was smitten — by the *resilience* emanating from that carefree laugh.

Prompted by the photo to find out more about Ritsos as a person, I read his sister Loula Ritsou-Glezou's book about their childhood in Monemvasia, where the poet was born in 1909. Loula describes how the menfolk played cards, went out hunting and visiting their properties, while the women stayed at home. The women in the Ritsos family, who could not find suitable husbands, spent their lives alone and probably dependent. Ritsos' mother was married at the age of twelve or thirteen; a year later, she was taken to Monemvasia, but she insisted on finishing her education at the Secondary School in Yithion, as their parents had agreed. A cultivated woman, her courageous and independent spirit became evident in her son Yannis, with whom she had a close relationship, and whose talent she recognised very early. The first of Ritsos' poems that I translated is *To tragoudi tis adelfismou* (*My sister's song*, here pp. 3–26).

Loula's description of their life in Monemvasia is echoed strongly in the collection of poems entitled *Tetarti Diastasi* (*The Fourth Dimension*), written between 1956 and 1972, in which Ritsos uses characters from Homer to explore what it means to be *fully* human, to achieve "the fourth dimension", or at least to realise that it exists. As a prelude to this selection, Ritsos includes *The Moonlight Sonata*.

The troubled and lonely woman in this dramatic monologue does not take on the persona of a mythical character. As the poem was published in 1956, she would have been born at the end of the nineteenth century. Her life has an echo of the somewhat circumscribed lives of women during that era.

The elderly woman begs the young man, who listens to her confession, to take her with him, away from her decaying house, which is reminiscent of the long-deserted house in Monemvasia. The harsh moonlight emphasises the disintegration inexorably taking place around her. She has achieved notable fame as a writer of religious verse, but, like the mythical characters in *The Fourth Dimension*, such as Ajax and Agamemnon, who realise that chasing after glory does not bring fulfilment, and is pointless, the elderly woman confesses that her poetic achievement "is not enough". She mentions that she was married, perhaps at a very young age. What she clearly sees now is the lack in her life of emotional fulfilment; in sacrificing all to her religious fervour and concentrating on her poetic achievement, she has landed herself in an impasse, a vacuum. In her feeling of helplessness, she identifies with the dancing bear in the poem, whose entrapment reflects Greece's neo-colonial situation after the war. The elderly woman has neither the strength nor the will to free herself from this impasse, caused by what Ritsos would define as a fatally attractive "selfish middle-class individualism".

In a tribute to Yannis Ritsos in the newspaper *Rizospastis* in 1989, the poet himself said:

If you are not a citizen — if you don't participate in the historical events of your country and of the world, it is as if you are a fugitive from life. You have nothing to live for. You can only pity these people, but not excuse them.

At the end of the poem, the young man leaves the house, as Ritsos says, with an ironic and perhaps compassionate smile on his face. His brief, loud, unrestrained laugh conveys a feeling of *liberation* after the lengthy confession. This carefree laugh, which, as Ritsos says, "is not unseemly beneath the moon", brings to mind the photograph on the record sleeve, while the moon continues to tempt the elderly woman away from involvement, and into escape and isolation. The young man soon falls silent and says "The decline of an era". He can do nothing for the elderly woman.

However, there is a glimmer of hope that she will leave the house, and engage with her fellow human beings in the town, with "its calloused hands, the town of the daily wage". Yet, against the nostalgic notes of Beethoven's music, which accompanies this monologue, the old lady will have to make a real effort to go out of the house.

This poem is probably the best known of Yannis Ritsos' poems. The poet himself mentioned to me that it had been translated many times. It is justifiably highly thought-of. It moves beyond the merely socio-political comment. Its theme — the corrosive effects of time and memory — has a universal appeal.

In 2002, I sent my translation of *The Moonlight Sonata* to the Gate Theatre in London, which specialises in translated plays. David Lane, then the Head Reader at the Gate Theatre, wrote the following comment:

> A beautiful and poignant poem on the decline of an era, and human deterioration through age, compared to the eternal nature of the written word. The powerful imagery is conjured up through her memories and the delicate language.

And now, after all these years, three students from my alma mater have kindly agreed to read this translation. I am also looking forward to hearing this beautiful poem presented in the original Greek.

INDEX OF TITLES AND FIRST LINES

Titles of poems are in italics, titles of collections or poems first published on their own are in italic capitals, and first lines of poems in upright type. Where a first line is very short the second line, or the first part of it, is also given; where a first line is very long, only the first part is given. Page numbers in square brackets in entries for titles indicate references to, or quotations from, the poem or collection in question which occur in the Introduction (roman numerals) or in the essays at the back of the book (page numbers 201ff). Where the only numbers against a title are in square brackets, that poem or collections will not be found among the poems that constitute the main part of the book. Alphabetization is by whole word, so that, for example, "He who…" precedes "Her name…". Titles and first lines that begin with an article are listed under "A", "An" or "The".

A big sky filled with swallows (Sachtouris) 174
A girl on the balcony dark hair unbraided (Ritsos) 109
A large rose / climbs companionless (Ritsos) 104
A pile of ancient books. / Darkened icons on the walls (Vafopoulos) 119
A ruined bell-tower / shows the road of fire (Gatsos) 141
A summer night (Gatsos) 140
A yard, a tree, a little sun in the morning on the wall (Ritsos) 79

Absent minded with love or *What does Emily Dickinson want of us?* (Kondos) 193
Ah, what a withered meadow (Gatsos) 140
Ajax 89–99 (Ritsos) [xii–xiii, 209, 224]
AMORGOS (Gatsos) 127–31 [xv]
An end to journeys (Kondos) 185
And those who have been killed for the dream (Vrettakos) 149
AT THE COMING OF DAY (Kondos) 185–9
Awake, clear running water from the pine tree root (Gatsos) 130

BALLADS (Sachtouris) 167–74
Bare trees. Bare trees. / Plains of stone. Mute villages (Gatsos) 135
Beat tambourines on the slopes. In this gorge (Gatsos) 138
Beauty (Sachtouris) 164
Because I took you / from your dark lair (Gatsos) 140
Behold, three full years / have passed now since (Vafopoulos) 113
Birds black arrows of intractable grief (Sachtouris) 172
Blood, blood, blood / desire iron smoke (Gatsos) 139

INDEX OF TITLES AND FIRST LINES

Bronze Age (Kondos) 192
CHORUS (Vrettakos) 151–159 [xvi]
Chorus (Vrettakos) 158
Church lit to its depths / above me (Vrettakos) 158
Consolatory (Ritsos) 108
Creation (Vrettakos) 157

DANGER IN THE STREETS (Kondos) [xvii]
Deep mine (Sachtouris) 171
Don't go away beast / beast with the iron teeth (Sachtouris) 175
Down in the white sea / I shall sleep the sleep of children (Gatsos) 139
During the course of his mysterious life man (Gatsos) 131

Empty bottles thrown in the yard (Ritsos) 106
Epigram of life (Vrettakos) 158
Erotic sleep after love. Damp sheets (Ritsos) 101
Euphoria (Vrettakos) 145
Every day I see him, as if for the first / time (Vrettakos) 158
Experiments for the repetition of night (Sachtouris) 176

Far away in another world this carnival took place (Sachtouris) 180
FAREWELL (Ritsos) 65–78 [x–xi, 220–21]
Fear (Vafopoulos) 117
First Symphony in Red and White (Vafopoulos) 123–4 [xiv]
Fishing village (Ritsos) 106
For schoolfellows (Kondos) 196
Fourteen poems for the same mountain (Vrettakos) 151–55
From the light of the golden beach in your eyes (Gatsos) 139

GIFTS IN ABEYANCE (Vrettakos) 145–9 [xvi]
God will have smiled once at the fire in your eye (Gatsos) 137

He sprinkled ugliness with beauty (Sachtouris) 164
He was holding his hat on his knee (Ritsos) 105
He who will come in the night may / be Jesus (Vrettakos) 148
He with the hat (Ritsos) 105
Helen (Ritsos) [207–08, 209]
Her name was Seashore and Sunday (Sachtouris) 169
How very much I loved you I alone know (Gatsos) 132

INDEX OF TITLES AND FIRST LINES

I climbed you up and down, carrying / the sky (Vrettakos) 152
I do not know where / the poems come from (Vrettakos) 157
I don't fear time / said the butcher to me (Kondos) 188
I gaze at nature. I am not calm (Kondos) 195
I had forgotten you, frightened little creature (Vafopoulos) 116
I have travelled struggling through many / winds (Vrettakos) 155
I know that you were before / I was born (Vrettakos) 157
I minister to the pain of life, but I must / not forge (Vrettakos) 147
I needed you to exist. To find / somewhere to rest my grief (Vrettakos) 155
I often try to fathom the depth / of insects' eyes (Vrettakos) 148
I promised the one who was all things (Vrettakos) 154
I reckon I have still a thousand / poems to write (Vrettakos) 157
I return to your old house (Kondos) 185
I saw the lightning, its snake-like / quiver (Vrettakos) 152
I spoke to you with the words of the shepherds (Vrettakos) 156
I tried hard this rough / weather (Vrettakos) 156
I want to weave, render in words / in the rhythm (Vrettakos) 156
I was ten years old when I carved / my name (Vrettakos) 154
In the yards of the afflicted the sun does not rise (Gatsos) 130
In this garden the roses were white (Vafopoulos) 123
Ioannis Veniamin d'Arkozi who died (Sachtouris) 167
Ismene (Ritsos) [214]
It could be a Bergman film (Kondos) 191
It is not the cloud that today (Vrettakos) 151
It isn't Oedipus (Sachtouris) 174

Justification (Ritsos) 107

LEND SILKEN THREADS TO THE WIND (Gatsos) 135–40 [xv]
Let me come with you. What a moon tonight (Ritsos) 57
Like the bee round a wild / flower, so am I (Vrettakos) 147
LOVE POEMS (Ritsos) 101–04

Memory of lost blood (Vrettakos) 149
MERCURIAL TIME (Kondos) [xvii]
Merope I close my eyes to remember the earth (Gatsos) 140
Metamorphosis (Sachtouris) 181
Mistaken identities (Kondos) 187
Morning, twilight. / A couple having breakfast (Kondos) 191
Musical substitute (Ritsos) 108

My friends are leaving / they've come to say goodbye (Sachtouris) 176
My sister / I should have stood upright (Ritsos) 3
MY SISTER'S SONG (Ritsos) 3–26 [ix–x, 224]

Neither (Vrettakos) 159
Neither loneliness nor the night / hold fear for me (Vrettakos) 159
Night harbour / lights drowned in the water (Ritsos) 27
Nostalgia returns (Sachtouris) 178
Not yet have I come to say farewell (Vrettakos) 151

Observatory (Sachtouris) 168
On the nature of the beast (Sachtouris) 175
On the one scale put the sun; / put the sea; put song (Vafopoulos) 115
On the table they had placed / a head of clay (Sachtouris) 177
On the wet streets of evening / a hazy blue light rises (Sachtouris) 165
One Anna brought me your news (Kondos) 186
One day I'll awake / as a star (Sachtouris) 181
One night (Ritsos) 107
Orange tree of Aegina (Gatsos) 139
Orestes (Ritsos) [204-05]
Out of superfluity (Vrettakos) 149

Paschal exhortation (Vrettakos) 159
Patient horses wait in the courtyard (Gatsos) 138
Pedagogics (Kondos) 194
Persephone (Ritsos) [214–15]
Phaedra (Ritsos) [212–14]
Philoctetes (Ritsos) [206–07]
Poetry (Vrettakos) 158
Poetry is: God / who marches (Vrettakos) 158
Put the wings — your blades / in their sheaths (Kondos) 193
Put your bare foot / on the paper (Ritsos) 104

RESPONSES (Ritsos) 105–109
Rural country (Kondos) 195

Scales (Vafopoulos) 115
SCRIPTURE OF THE BLIND (Ritsos) [208–209]
Short ode (Vrettakos) 146
Sitting opposite my gracious / mountain, I consider (Vrettakos) 146

INDEX OF TITLES AND FIRST LINES

Sometimes a bird comes out of the cloud (Sachtouris) 173
Sometimes the women (Sachtouris) 173
SONGS OF RESURRECTION (Vafopoulos) 119–22
Spanish Rhapsody (Gatsos) 135–6
Spring Symphony (Ritsos) [x]
Sudden charge (Ritsos) 106

Take your ring (Gatsos) 137
That white face, / dyed with white lead (Kondos) 189

The ambulances passed in the night sounding their horns (Ritsos) 107
The anatomist (Kondos) 188

THE BIG NIGHT AND THE WINDOW (Vafopoulos) 115–17
The black, carved desk, the two silver candlesticks (Ritsos) 87
The blood (Ritsos) 105

The calendar (Vafopoulos) 113-14 [xiv]
The carnival (Sachtouris) 180 [xvi–xvii]
The cloud (Vrettakos) 151

The dead house (Ritsos) [201–204, 205, 209–10]
The dead man in our lives Ioannis Veniamin d'Arkozi (Sachtouris) 167
The decay of hands (Vrettakos) 148
The dream (Sachtouris) 163-4

The eternal dream / caresses its white hair (Sachtouris) 163
The excavations showed your inauspicious / mornings (Kondos) 192
The eyes of insects (Vrettakos) 148

The field of words (Vrettakos) 147
THE FORGOTTEN WOMAN (Sachtouris) 163–5
THE FOURTH DIMENSION (Ritsos) 89–99 [xii, 201–215, 217, 224]

The gifts (Sachtouris) 170
The Greek language (Vrettakos) 146

The heavenly lace of your outlines (Vrettakos) 153
The hedgehog (Vafopoulos) 116
The hour of waiting (Ritsos) 109

The last swallow, a black band on the sleeve (Ritsos) 108
The lies are over at last — ours and theirs (Ritsos) 66
The lorries passed raising dust (Ritsos) 105

231

INDEX OF TITLES AND FIRST LINES

THE MARCH OF THE OCEAN (Ritsos) 27–56 [x]
THE MOONLIGHT SONATA (Ritsos) 57–64 [x, xi, 217–18, 223–5]

The nightmare (Sachtouris) 169 [xvii]
THE NOTHING ATHLETE (Kondos) 191–196

THE OFFERING (Vafopoulos) 113–14

The plan was greater, Lord (Vrettakos) 149
The poet's room (Ritsos) 87
The poor houses of fishermen, roofs, smoke-stained doors (Ritsos) 106
THE PRISON TREE AND THE WOMEN (Ritsos) 79–85 [xi–xii, 218–20]

The return of Iphigeneia (Ritsos) [208]

The scene (Sachtouris) 177
THE SEQUEL (Vafopoulos) 123–124
The sky (Sachtouris) 172
The sky blows golden light / into things (Vrettakos) 159
The sponge-divers slept under the big clock of the customs house (Ritsos) 107
The sunset gleamed / on the body of a bird (Ritsos) 103

The telephone (Sachtouris) 179
The Ten Commandments (Vrettakos) 147
The three lovers (Sachtouris) 165
The traveller with the black box (Kondos) 189
The tulip (Vrettakos) 148

The woman undressed and lay on the bed (Sachtouris) 178
The workshop (Vrettakos) 157

Their country lashed to the sails / and the oars hanging (Gatsos) 127
Therefore I turn the stone of the ring inwards, I clasp it (Ritsos) 102
These (Ritsos) 109
These look sideways, always suspicious (Ritsos) 109
They say that the mountains shake and the fir trees are angry (Gatsos) 127
They're temporarily lost, they've become shadows (Kondos) 196
Thieves of the sun / they never once saw a green bough (Sachtouris) 168
This evening my soul ascended, a full moon / rising (Vrettakos) 145
This loneliness and this silence are not / the old loneliness (Vafopoulos) 117
Thou in me (Vafopoulos) 119–22 [xiv]
Tired people wait smoking, / outside events (Ritsos) 108
To bring you herbs and myrrh (Gatsos) 136

INDEX OF TITLES AND FIRST LINES

Today I put on a / warm red blood (Sachtouris) 170
Tree planting (Vrettakos) 146
TWELVE POEMS ON CAVAFY (Ritsos) 87
Twenty-four-hour news (Kondos) 186
Two girls gazed at me / eanestly and spoke to me (Kondos) 187

Under the shadow of the mountain (Ritsos) [201–03]
Up here death is unknown (Vrettakos) 153

We're phoning / about a dead man (Sachtouris) 179
What became of Charles Dickens's children (Kondos) 196
What can you say? Virgins stoop (Gatsos) 136
What has become of those hands that made / stone into beauty (Vrettakos) 148
Whatever happens (Vrettakos) 145
Whatever happens, I will not deny / the world (Vrettakos) 145
When I came into the world and saw / the sun (Vrettakos) 152
When I sometime leave this light / I shall meander upwards (Vrettakos) 146
WITH FACE TO THE WALL (Sachtouris) 175–81
With fear I write to you from an all-night arcade (Sachtouris) 171
Woman, what are you staring at? Close the doors (Ritsos) 89
Words are the tree on which / my soul branches out (Vrettakos) 146

You must wash your hands. / You must eat up your food (Kondos) 194
You threw off the sheets / you opened the windows (Ritsos) 103
Your body on the beach / the sand clinging to your flesh (Ritsos) 102
Your snows were false / my friends (Kondos) 196
You've come back from the market blithely carrying (Ritsos) 101

Ingram Content Group UK Ltd.
Milton Keynes UK
UKHW021455160323
418667UK00010B/851